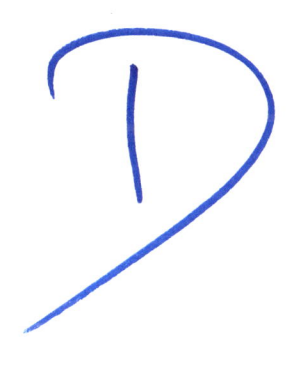

The Whitford Way

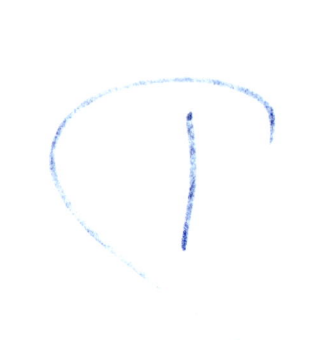

The Whitford Way

A STORY OF CORPORATE CHEMISTRY IN THE REAL WORLD

*The most remarkable company
you are probably unaware of
whose products influence
so many aspects of your daily life*

Tony Tedeschi

© 2017 Whitford Worldwide Company

All rights reserved.

ISBN: 1539179222
ISBN 13: 9781539179221
Library of Congress Control Number: 2016916614
CreateSpace Independent Publishing Platform
North Charleston, South Carolina

References to the following trademarked products appear in the narrative:

General Trademarks: George Foreman Grill®, Kleenex®, Nylon®, Salton®, Toastmaster®, Tootsie Roll®

Registered trademarks of DuPont®: Chemours®, Teflon®, TeflonS®, Freon®, SilverStone®

Registered trademarks of Whitford®: Whitford Chemical®, BlisterGuard®, Eclipse®, Eterna®, EterniTex®, Excalibur®, GlidePath®, Kneadatite®, QuanTanium®, Resilon®, Tetran®, Whitcon®, Xylan®

**This
Changes
Everything**

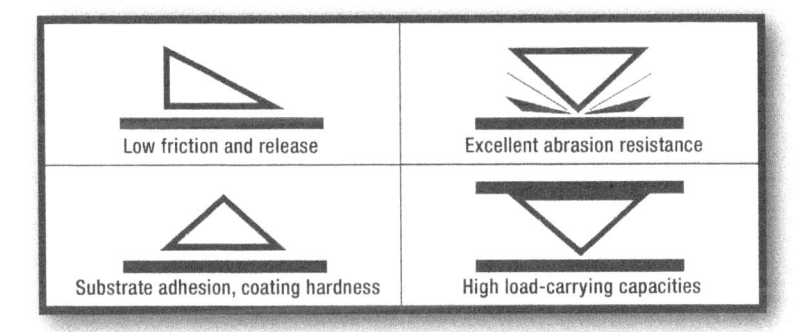

Low friction and release	Excellent abrasion resistance
Substrate adhesion, coating hardness	High load-carrying capacities

Making the world run more smoothly . . .

Whitford products make automobiles quieter, oil rigs safer, wind turbines more efficient, and cookware easier to clean. Yet few people recognize the name. Here is the story of the company's first fifty years—the human side of building a great business. Whether you're a high school teacher, a surgeon, or Harvard's newest MBA, this is definitely worth reading.

—Joseph J. Dunn, Author, After One Hundred Years: Corporate Profits, Wealth, and American Society

The Whitford story serves as an important lesson in how a relentlessly competitive global market leader doesn't have to abandon the sleeves-rolled-up values that were so vital to building the business. This informative, intimate retrospective reveals with engaging detail how Whitford chemistry is about much more than the innovative science behind its products that makes a difference in everyone's lives. Whitford chemistry is also about its people and how they, too, make a difference.

—Peter Giannetti, Editor-in-Chief, HomeWorld Business

It seems impossible that a company as successful as Whitford could be so little known to end-users. For more than 50 years, Whitford has challenged so many of the "tried-and-true" business theories, while customizing its business to real world problem solutions. While "The Whitford Way" is a great case study for business students interested in challenges to conventional wisdom, its real value is as a blueprint for anyone starting a business, especially its unique approaches to dealing with shoe-string advertising budgets and selling during economic downturns.

—Joe Quinlan, President, Restore Automotive Products

After starting five companies over a career of forty-plus years, I have recently focused on helping early stage companies get a start. As "The Whitford Way" chronicles, many successful companies "boot-strapped" their growth without the luxury of easy external money and the Internet. They grew by being accountable to customers and fulfilling promises to suppliers. The best deals are often made over a handshake that is a warranty with a promise to either deliver or make the other party whole. This dinosaur's reading of "The Whitford Way" was a wonderful validation for the core principles and hard work that have been the root of his foundation and success.

—*Coley Brown, Founder and CEO, VisionMine.com*

*This book is dedicated to all the wonderful people
who have made Whitford the success it is today.*

*The author would like to thank Joan Eberhardt of Whitford for applying
her vast knowledge of the company to provide invaluable advice and
assistance with this project.*

Contents

Preface · xiii

Introduction · xv

Chapter 1 Why the Whitford Way? · · · · · · · · · · · · · · · · · · · 1

Chapter 2 In the Beginning · 16

Chapter 3 Xylan Launches a Company · · · · · · · · · · · · · · · · 33

Chapter 4 The Early Years Begin to Define a Company · · · 45

Chapter 5 How to Survive a Meltdown · · · · · · · · · · · · · · · 64

Chapter 6 How to Keep It Going · · · · · · · · · · · · · · · · · · · 75

Chapter 7 Modern-Day Alchemy…but This Time It Works · · · 91

Chapter 8 Silent Partners on the Road · · · · · · · · · · · · · · 108

Chapter 9 Energy's Shifting Winds · · · · · · · · · · · · · · · · · 124

Chapter 10	Building the Business of Cookware and Bakeware	142
Chapter 11	Thinking outside the Box...or Not	163
Chapter 12	Developing a Different Business Approach	180
Chapter 13	Creating and Building a Consistent Brand Identity	192
Chapter 14	Recruiting and Retaining the Whitford Way	211
Chapter 15	A Long-Established Global Presence	228
Chapter 16	The Customer Is Always...	244
Chapter 17	Xylan's Extended Family	260
Chapter 18	That Uniquely Whitford Way	269
	Epilogue	275
	Endpaper	279
	Index	281

Preface

In 2014, I was hired by Dave Willis, the CEO of Whitford Worldwide, to help with a history of the company, which is the manufacturer of the world's largest, most complete line of fluoropolymer coatings for industrial and consumer industries. Whitford coatings are on everything from frying pans to the nuts and bolts on oil rigs, and piston skirts in automobiles, even fabric for athletic socks. Whitford would be celebrating its fiftieth anniversary in 2015, and Willis had a manuscript the company had commissioned. However, he had issues with it and was looking for a professional writer/editor to address them.

He connected with me via the editor of *HomeWorld Business*, the leading trade publication in the housewares and home furnishings industry. My assignment was to prepare the existing manuscript for a limited publication run to be distributed to employees, former employees, customers, and suppliers, principally people with whom Whitford interacted.

While working my way through the existing manuscript, I had a number of meetings with Willis and was in repeated contact with him via telephone and e-mail. As I got deeper and deeper into what had been written and learned more and more about Whitford, what the company produced, and how it operated, my experience as a journalist, business writer, and author led me to conclude this was a story of much broader interest.

Whitford is a company that affects the lives of millions of people on a daily basis, but its coatings have little to no brand identity among end users, even in terms of popular consumer items such as cookware and bakeware. The effects of its coatings reduce friction on products and the components of products in so many areas of our lives that the company has a demonstrably beneficial effect on how the world works. As more and more aspects of this story began to unfold, I found myself editing less and writing more. I asked Willis to let me run with this for a while and see where it led. That came to involve more than sixty interviews with staff, former employees, customers, and media.

While Whitford has underwritten my work, I was allowed complete editorial integrity. The result is *The Whitford Way*, a compelling story of the entrepreneurial spirit at work.

INTRODUCTION

In 1970, barely a year into the existence of Whitford Corporation, Dave Willis, the company's cofounder, made a trip to a new client in Southern California to deal with a problem with a Whitford product, a nonstick coating for crepe pans. The coating was coming loose from the cooking surface and turning a chalk white. An analysis showed that the engineer who had written the client's specifications had underestimated the heat on the surface of the pan by two hundred degrees Fahrenheit—that is, it was not a problem with the coating but with the specification for the level of heat the coating needed to withstand.

Armed with the new spec, Willis returned to his company headquarters. His chemist reformulated the coating to meet the new spec; however, just solving the problem and shipping the new formula to the customer would not satisfy Willis's sense of how a customer should be treated.

"Dave and one of his engineers flew out and spent a couple of days with us to figure out how to make this material work," the customer explained. "They knew it would have the temperature resistance but were not real sure what the pretreatment would be. Together, we figured that all out."

The customer has been a Whitford client ever since.

While the successful application of a nonstick coating onto a pan used to make crepes was never going to have a significant impact on how the world turns, the attention to solving the problem at all levels of the operation became fundamental to how Whitford does business, and that has had a major impact on people's lives via a vast array of industries. For a half century, Whitford has indeed been deeply involved in making the world a better place to live.

Whitford has grown to become the manufacturer of the world's largest, most complete line of fluoropolymer coatings for industrial and consumer industries. With a presence in countries around the world, including research and development labs, manufacturing facilities, and sales offices, Whitford produces coatings that address the needs of a nearly incalculable number of products, from the nuts and bolts that hold an oil rig together to the coating on a rice cooker in an Asian restaurant, the fabric in a marathoner's athletic socks to the cylinders and pistons in all manner of vehicles, legions of cookware and bakeware products, medical instruments, and on and on. Simply listing the applications would fill chapters in this book and not account for new applications being developed while those chapters were being written.

Although Whitford is a company that affects the lives of millions of people on a daily basis, it is generally a supplier to coating applicators and equipment manufacturers that sell the final product—that is, two steps removed from the customer.

Nonetheless, Whitford's reputation among the companies it supplies is stellar, with cadres of customers that have been loyal purchasers for decades.

Suffice to say "The Whitford Way" is much more than a formula for uniquely successful chemistry. It is the chemistry for how to run a successful, universally impactful company.

CHAPTER 1

WHY THE WHITFORD WAY?

An entrepreneurial culture is an environment where someone is motivated to innovate, create and take risks.
—REFERENCE.COM

"Entrepreneurial" is perhaps the most revered adjective used to describe an American company. But what are the characteristics of that company? How does "entrepreneurial" really work? Start a company with an idea. Experiment with making the idea into something real. Target the markets for the products that result. Build a company around those products. Continue to expand the product line to grow the business, eventually selling into markets worldwide. Sometimes, even change the way the world works.

Welcome to the Whitford way.

In a modern business world, where there are endless examples of people finding ways to game the system, the story of Whitford is the classic definition of "entrepreneurial" put into practice.

Whitford is one of those American business success stories with very modest beginnings. It is a corporation built the way American companies are supposed to be built, from the ground up, its original facility a converted garage. Its predecessor company, Whitford Chemical, was founded in 1965 by Dave Willis and Ted Rehmeyer, both of whom had been recently let go by Liquid Nitrogen Processing, a chemical company. But Willis, who had been the sales manager at LNP, was convinced he could beat his former employer at its own game. After more than a half century, Willis's conviction has long since been validated—and then some. Whitford is, today, the manufacturer of the largest, most complete line of fluoropolymer coatings, with operations worldwide.

Whitford coatings have a universal impact on everyday life, although they are almost never recognized as such. Most often they are completely invisible to those who benefit from them. These engineered coatings lack the sex appeal of the glitzy accoutrements that are the stars in today's world, those high-tech must-haves that have proliferated everywhere and seem to become outdated before you discard the box they came in. Nonetheless, Whitford coatings are no less important to the way the world works. And while high-tech glam objects are the definition of programmed obsolescence, Whitford products have made an art form of longevity. Some of Whitford's earliest products are still selling well today.

Your Car and So Much More

New vehicle models are striking examples of where the contrasting technologies conjoin. More and more passenger cars, SUVs, and trucks have become multiton computers on wheels, with new technology creating pathways by which even drivers appear headed for obsolescence. But laboring behind and beneath the flashy onboard dashboard computers are the components that keep the show on the road, literally. And they continue to do so long after a vehicle is traded in for the latest high-tech model.

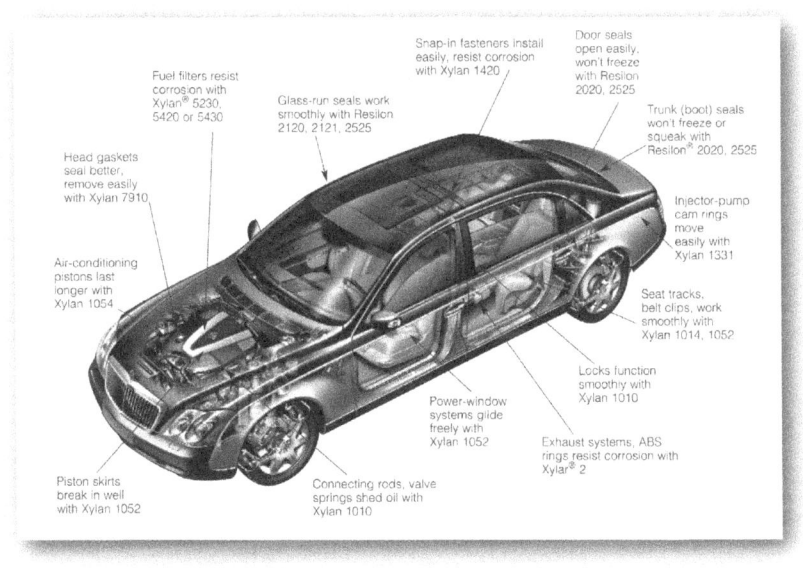

[Diagram of a car with callouts:
- Fuel filters resist corrosion with Xylan® 5230, 5420 or 5430
- Snap-in fasteners install easily, resist corrosion with Xylan 1420
- Door seals open easily, won't freeze with Resilon 2020, 2525
- Glass-run seals work smoothly with Resilon 2120, 2121, 2525
- Trunk (boot) seals won't freeze or squeak with Resilon® 2020, 2525
- Head gaskets seal better, remove easily with Xylan 7910
- Injector-pump cam rings move easily with Xylan 1331
- Air-conditioning pistons last longer with Xylan 1054
- Seat tracks, belt clips, work smoothly with Xylan 1014, 1052
- Locks function smoothly with Xylan 1010
- Power-window systems glide freely with Xylan 1052
- Piston skirts break in well with Xylan 1052
- Connecting rods, valve springs shed oil with Xylan 1010
- Exhaust systems, ABS rings resist corrosion with Xylar® 2]

Whitford coatings make every car last longer, look better and run more efficiently

Whitford coatings are essential to the operation of engine parts and numerous other components throughout the auto body. When the pistons in your car seize up without their Whitford coatings, pray that your acrobatic body language can direct your car to the road shoulder without its Whitford-assisted steering components. And, oh, you'll have to pray you roll to a stop before the downslope of the hill without your Whitford-assisted braking. If you finally do manage to bring the car safely

3

to a halt, let's hope it is not on one of those brutally hot and humid summer days, because without Whitford coatings, your air conditioner would not be working.

So without the super-slippery goop that pours out of the vats at Whitford locations around the world, the machine would grind to a halt, becoming a very expensive static display.

For many auto models, Whitford coatings also enhance the pleasure of the driving experience. If you drive a vehicle built by Ford, General Motors, Mercedes, Toyota, Suzuki, Kia, Hyundai, Nissan, or Volkswagen, the quiet of your ride is largely the result of Whitford noise-reduction coatings used throughout models built by these companies. They also provide for the squeak-free glide of your windows within their channel runs.

But your car is just one example of Whitford's reach into your world. As you walk from room to room in your house, Whitford is the silent partner in your daily routine. Whitford coatings are there on your kitchen cookware and bakeware, your coffeemaker, your knives, the steam iron for your clothes, the curling iron for your hair. They are out back on your barbecue grill, your garden shears, your pruners, and your mower blades.

Whitford coatings enhance the fabric on your luggage, on the seating of your outdoor furniture, even in your athletic socks and some of the clothes on your back. They are on belts in your treadmill at the gym, the copier or reprographic roller in your home office copy machine, and the larger one cranking out pages at the office.

The gas or oil you use to heat your home is produced with the help of thousands of Whitford-coated components, at work throughout the process of oil and gas production. If you are benefitting from wind-powered energy, components in the giant windmills are Whitford coated.

Your life also is enhanced indirectly by many, many Whitford-coated commercial products. They are on the cookware at your favorite gourmet restaurant and the rice cooker at your favorite Asian restaurant. They enhance the usefulness of bakeware at your local bakery or the bakery department at your supermarket, where the Whitford coating has such an effective release point, a cake falls out of its mold before the baker can tilt it to vertical.

The list goes on and on and on. Indeed, it is hard to imagine a day in your life that you are not in touch with Whitford somewhere along the way.

Unique Business Personality

What is so special about this company you know little or nothing about? Is there a formula for its success and the incredible reach of its products? While Whitford may be little known outside its business universe, it has grown into a highly respected, multinational corporation within an industry of competitive Goliaths. It has done this without ever losing focus on its unique business personality.

At the heart of Whitford's compelling success story is a business model uniquely its own. It would be difficult to assert that there could be anything truly unique about the individual elements of running a business today. How a company stitches those elements together, however, creates its particular corporate personality. It can be seen in how the company recruits and then trains new employees. It is a factor in what it expects of them on the job, how it rewards them, and how they advance within the corporate structure. It bears on why they decide to stay or to move on. It is there, as well, in how the company's personnel connect with suppliers, customers, competitors, the media—really anyone who has reason to interact with the company. All these elements are significant to companies small, medium, and large; local, nationwide, global; manufacturing products, selling services, providing financing, and so on.

Whitford's success is not simply a matter of its many, many patents and the breadth of its product line. It's a reflection of its unique business model, a modus operandi that makes customers throughout the world feel connected, feel that they are being handled on a personal level and that their specific needs generate specific solutions.

One of the most overused phrases on business pages for the past several years has been "too big to fail." Implicit in that description is a sense that size is what distinguishes truly successful corporations. But while that sense of size also implies that these corporations touch us in many ways, throughout our daily lives, size often results in impersonal relationships.

So much of business reporting also involves billion-dollar initial public offerings of dot-coms, many of which haven't come close to turning a profit and don't have prospects for doing so any time soon. Other dominant stories involve Wall Street investment houses or hedge funds that seem to do little more than move money around at great profit.

Brian Willis, Whitford's specialist in engineering technology for Xylan coatings, spent years working with the oil and gas industry.

What can be said of Whitford, over its fifty-year-plus existence, is that it is the right size to succeed. That it is a company where, day in and day out, products come out the door and ship to customers all over the world. What Whitford has been able to do, that giant corporations selling off-the-shelf products are often reluctant to do, is tailor its products to specific customer needs. That sort of tailoring is something Whitford does with a vengeance.

"Working with the oil and gas industry, we employ specification selling to solving problems," said Brian Willis, a senior sales executive at Whitford. "It all starts with a company that is having an issue. For example, it can be a problem with adhesion, friction, or corrosion due to long-term exposure to weather or seawater. We coat a sample part and return it to the customer. When the coating performs well, we have a new customer."

"Inside" or "Outside"

To ensure that customers understand, Whitford takes a high level of ongoing, very personal interest in providing specific solutions to specific needs. Whitford personnel spend a lot of time and energy traveling. They conduct sit-downs with customers on virtually every continent. They do this in a global business environment in which the face of your customer or your prospect is more likely to be on a computer screen at your headquarters than on the other side of a table. With so much business being conducted via teleconference, Skype, e-mail, e-chats, and so forth, this emphasis on personal service also sets the company apart.

"The shift away from face-to-face selling is driving many top companies to hire and cultivate people who can become subject-matter experts and communicate with customers with a combination of e-mail, phone, texting, social media, and Web conferencing," Geoffrey James wrote in an article on the website *Inc.com* in February 2013.[1]

However, Lynette Ryals, writing in the *Harvard Business Review*, said it is face-to-face "transactional selling" that is dead, emphasizing the importance of selling value versus selling product.

"Increasingly, customers resent having to spend time in sales calls purely to make standard transactions," she writes. "Successful

---
[1] "Selling Face to Face Is Almost Obsolete," Geoffrey James, Inc.com, February 8, 2013, http://www.inc.com/geoffrey-james/selling-face-to-face-is-almost-obsolete.html.

salespeople focus on the value that their products and services add to the customer...Of course they have a thorough knowledge of their company and its offerings, but they apply that knowledge to the customer's specific issues and problems."[2]

Ryals could very well be writing a page for a Whitford sales manual.

Research bears out these shifts in how selling is conducted. A 2009 survey for the US Travel Association (USTA) found that business leaders estimated face-to-face selling (outside sales) converted an impressive 40 percent of prospects to customers. Virtual selling (inside sales) converted just 16 percent. In other words, face-to-face selling closed 2.5 times better than remote selling. While a similar survey conducted in 2012 found inside sales increasing their conversions to 23 percent, face-to-face selling held its own, even gaining a few points at 42 percent.

With company growth and the ever-evolving technical communications revolution, inside sales also evolved along with these trends.

"Many years ago when we were much smaller, anyone could answer these incoming sales and technical calls," Brian Willis said. "Out of convenience, these were considered 'tech calls' and sent to the laboratory, where any available technician would answer them. No logging, follow-up, et cetera. Then the lab would just send out coating samples to move the process along."

In 2001, when Brian Willis started at inside sales, he began documenting the categories of the calls.

---
[2] Lynette Ryals, "Make the Most of Your Sales Call," *Harvard Business Review*, June 29, 2012.

"One-third were new potential customers," he said, "one-third existing customers looking for a coating recommendation for a new application, one-third actually asking a technical question about an existing coating. I kept asking, 'Then why are these called tech calls?'"

He was sure CEO Dave Willis would not be happy if he knew that two-thirds of the incoming "tech calls" were in fact sales calls and not going to the sales department, being logged in, or followed up on.

Today, Whitford has full-time inside salespeople, fully engaged with phone calls, e-mails, and inquiries from advertising programs with industry-specific websites.

"Inside sales also supports the outside-sales effort as their feet on the ground at headquarters," Brian Willis explained. "In my specific assignment, I also support the outside-sales efforts of our affiliates worldwide. I see this as the new way of doing business. Customers have already decided what they want before they even contact you. Outside sales then facilitates the sale, making personal contact with the customer."

The USTA surveys also indicated that some companies tightened their belts during the lean years following the onset of recession in late 2007. However, those companies, like Whitford, that did not cut back on outside selling gained customers at the expense of rivals who severely restricted employee travel.

A Sense of Family
Across its fifty-year history, Whitford's reach has expanded to include facilities around the world. This worldwide expansion

could cause a company to become disengaged from day-to-day concerns for the people who work throughout these far-flung locations. In Whitford's case, however, the effective achievement of such an expansion is, to a significant degree, a result of precisely the way people at the company are treated. The company promotes a strong sense of family—from the top down—with the attendant deep feelings of loyalty that attitude engenders.

In the words of a manager at Whitford's India operation, it is "the feeling of being part of this organization, where I can count my contribution in its growth and progress. The wide access and openness of the people pulls me in."

Calling it a sense of family may sound like a stretch, but "family" is a word often used by Whitford employees to describe their relationship to the company.

In comments on *Work Rules!*—a business bestseller by Laszlo Bock of Google—one reviewer wrote, "Bock also provides teaching examples from a range of industries—including companies that are household names but hideous places to work and little-known companies that achieve spectacular results by valuing and listening to their employees." [3]

At Whitford, an emphasis on listening to and valuing employees originated at the very top of the chain of command from the very outset. Dave Willis, Whitford's cofounder and its president for more than fifty years, maintained a deep understanding of the roles played by people in the organization. Along with his intimate understanding of all aspects of the company's operation, Willis was also extremely effective at using human resources.

---

3 Laszlo Bock, Work Rules! (New York, NY, 12, Hachette Book Group, 2015)

This Whitford group shot was taken in 1989. Dave Willis refers to it as Mrs. Ficca's 2nd grade class.

Paul Fields, the chemist who created Whitford's first product, said of him, "When Dave Willis sees a challenge, he has an innate ability to pick the appropriate people to meet it."

"You can do it" is the phrase Whitford staff members repeat over and over again. They use it when explaining how Willis encouraged them to address an issue or take on a management position they felt might be too daunting for their particular talents.

While Whitford is indeed represented with locations on five continents, it has fewer than seven hundred employees. Whitford retains a small-company feel with an unusually high employee allegiance. Whitford employees tend to stay for a long time; indeed, it is not unusual for people to leave Whitford, work for another company, and, after a time, return to Whitford.

What prompts this level of loyalty?

Is it seeing the potential in the young woman working for a customer in Australia and convincing her that she could manage the Whitford sales operation for Australia and New Zealand? Is it continually incenting her to move into more and more senior positions, until she became the company's major player in the entire Asia/Pacific region?

"Whitford was so much more than a company," she said. "A family comes to mind but not a family I had ever experienced."

Is it the culture shock of a new management employee in Germany watching the company president cleaning out a deep-fat fryer for display at an international trade show?

"Is this a hands-on company or what?" he exclaimed.

Is it cases like those of three German women who returned from positions at other companies because they "liked the family atmosphere that we shared with Whitford"?

Just a few of countless such examples about being an important, valued part of a larger whole.

Work Hard/Play Hard

The sense of belonging also extends beyond the workday relationships. "Work hard/play hard" is definitely a corporate mantra at Whitford. Retaining the ability to laugh at and with others, and

13

at oneself, is a common thread that has helped define Whitford. Laughter is crucial to the camaraderie that binds the people of Whitford. There are many stories of employees finding humor in and around the edges of working for Whitford, whether in lighter moments on the job; at corporate meetings; traveling on behalf of the company; or while interacting with clients, potential clients, vendors, even the media. One could say that work hard/play hard is an integral ingredient in the corporate chemistry. It is part of the history of how the company moves product and how it gains, holds, and sometimes loses customers. It is even apparent in the company's growth and how it has planted the Whitford flag in countries throughout the world.

So impactful is the work hard/play hard attitude at Whitford that in 2015, as part of the celebration of its golden anniversary, the company produced a "Whitford by Whitford Scrapbook," depicting, in words and photos, the lighter side of the corporate personality over the years. If other companies throw the perfunctory holiday season party and the summer barbecue, Whitford's attitude toward play is that it forms an integral part of the company's personality.

Work at Whitford requires intensity on the part of its employees. There is deep concentration involved in the development of one-of-a-kind formulae in the laboratory, as well as analyzing those formulae in quality control. There are the demands of pushing product out the door, creating marketing programs for target audiences, selling product during business trips, and so on. Critical to that effort is developing and reinforcing the camaraderie that is a key to the company's success.

Paramount among the reasons why the Whitford model works is an understanding that business is not about reaching a final destination. With the right team, with employees confident their work is valued, every new sale, every customized product delivered, every accomplishment sets up the next challenge.

Work takes up the better part of people's lifetimes. Work should not be about slogging through some job until you get to retire forty or fifty years down the road. That emphasizes the importance of choosing work that satisfies, challenges, even provides enjoyment, and leaves time for some play. What does a company that satisfies those objectives look like? Read on.

CHAPTER 2

IN THE BEGINNING

*The way to get started is to quit
talking and begin doing.*
—WALT DISNEY

Whitford Corporation is headquartered in Elverson, Pennsylvania, a tiny town of just over twelve hundred citizens, set in the eastern part of the state, some fifty miles from Philadelphia. Once off the Pennsylvania Turnpike, a visitor approaches the town down country roads, past rolling hills, thick woodlands, cornfields, and houses spotted here and there, until they congregate in small groupings around the center of town. Making a hard right turn off Park Avenue into the company's parking lot, you confront Whitford's stone-and-spired exterior suddenly looming over you with the look of a chateau, as if in defiance of the glass-box shapes of modern corporations and manufacturing facilities. A visitor immediately senses that this company swims against the current.

If you have a few moments in the lobby while the receptionist notifies your appointment, you are drawn to a display wall of

THE WHITFORD WAY

products whose manufacture is greatly influenced by Whitford chemistry: applications for all manner of industries and diverse consumer products such as cookware, bakeware, small electrics, even textiles, as well as the automotive, oil and gas, and aerospace industries. The display encapsulates decades of innovation by a company whose employees are the embodiment of a bias for action, the practice of which begins at the very top.

Dave Willis shown here in front of Whitford display wall.

Whitford chairman David P. Willis, Jr. is quick to point out that, while he is the cofounder of the company and its point man since then, he credits many employees, both past and present, for having made the company the success it is today. A good deal of that success is a result of the company's dogged pursuit of innovative products and its emphasis on providing solutions to customers' specific requirements. Long-term success is a matter of people at Whitford recognizing opportunities their competitors have overlooked or decided were not cost effective. Willis, on the other hand, is not a man to pass up a challenge, and his pursuit of opportunities has driven how the company operates, from research and development, through marketing and sales, to delivery of the products Whitford creates.

From a person's initial contact with Willis, it becomes apparent that he is a born salesman, but that initial impression also belies any image of a huckster just pushing a product at you. Willis is, first and foremost, a problem solver. When he and, by extension, Whitford have taken a significant step toward solving a customer's problem, then the process moves toward finalizing the sale.

Seated at his desk at Whitford, Willis sketched, on a piece of paper torn from a notepad, a graphic explanation of a chemical transformation. The exercise, in response to an interviewer's question, is perhaps the antithesis of sophisticated, computer-assisted design, but the drawing and Willis's explanation made a complex point easily understood.

That's not to say Whitford does not have its complement of the latest technology. Down the hall from Willis's office, on the second floor of the company's headquarters, is a state-of-the art meeting room—the corporate "War Room"—that looks as if it could provide the wherewithal to plan and launch drone strikes. Whitford labs and quality-control departments around the world are equipped with an expansive array of state-of-the-art, research-grade instrumentation.

"A Two-Car Garage"

Whitford's corporate headquarters is in sharp contrast to the garage in West Chester, Pennsylvania, where Willis and the company's cofounder, Ted Rehmeyer, drew up plans for their new company in 1965.

"A two-car garage," Willis said with a smile, as if to draw a contrast to the legendary tales of US business successes that began in…one-car garages.

Whitford's original West Chester facility (then); Whitford's current headquarters in Elverson, PA (now).

Willis is also not a man who will pass up having an edge. The edge for him came in an unexpected way.

Fresh out of the University of Pennsylvania's Wharton School, he went to work for Owens Corning Fiberglas to sell textile fibers. It was a seemingly odd choice for a graduate of a school with more than its fair share of future executives in more glamorous careers as investment bankers and stockbrokers.

"It was 1957," Willis explained. "Not a good year for jobs."

Indeed. A downturn begun in late 1957 and carrying through most of 1958 was the most significant recession, up to that point, of the post–World War II years. The US Bureau of Labor Statistics reported the unemployment rate, which had held steady between 4 percent and 4.5 percent throughout 1956 and most of 1957, topped 5 percent for the first time in November of 1957. That began a protracted increase, topping out at 7.5 percent the following August, before a slow decline into the fifth percentile in 1959. New-car sales fell 31 percent in 1958 versus 1957, new housing construction fell precipitously, durable-goods manufacturers were hit particularly hard, as were the lumber, mining, and textile industries. More than two million jobs were lost.

Secure in his job at Owens Corning as the economy improved, Willis was presented an opportunity with one of its customers, Liquid Nitrogen Processing, and he was lured away to become sales manager. LNP was also looking for an accountant, and Willis connected the company with Ted Rehmeyer, a fraternity brother at Phi Gamma Delta when both were at the University of Pennsylvania.

In spite of its name, LNP was principally a compounder of DuPont's Teflon dry resins, adding fillers and reinforcing agents to make materials, which were then sold to fabricators who made those resins into shapes used as seals, bearings, rods, and other forms that eventually made their way into general industry. They also compounded other plastic and thermoplastic resins with fillers similar to those used in the Teflon compounding operation. This was a new business, and it was growing rapidly. On the other hand, LNP was small enough that Willis was pretty much covering the entire United States. In the process, he grew the company's annual sales from $400,000 to $3 million in just five years, the equivalent of $22 million in 2016 dollars. But...

"I had become crosswise with the chairman and principal shareholder," Willis said. "We had a disagreement with the way I was promoting the company. He insisted I was wasting company money by spending $30,000 on ads to support my sales efforts. He fired me for being extravagant."

Whitford co-founder Ted Rehmeyer.

Ditto, Ted Rehmeyer. Three days before Christmas, 1964.

"We were both fired at the same time on December 22," Willis said. "So we both needed something to do. We each looked for a job for a few months, tried to buy something together but could not afford anything we found. I had four kids to support. Although Ted was not married, he wanted to get a master's degree, but agreed he could do the books, and what little administration was needed, part time."

They just needed a place to employ their talents.

Competing with a Former Employer

Having little money but knowing the Teflon compounding business, the two decided they could compete with their former employer. Ironically, they sold their shares in LNP to help finance their startup, also adding some personal savings. Willis's father bought some shares in the newly formed company and later advanced money in exchange for debentures. In effect, without any collateral except the promise to repay, he lent the company money that was used as working capital as the business grew. It was critical to their plans that the new business did not require a lot of capital at the time.

"The new business seemed like a good idea that used both of our skills," Willis recalled. "I had been selling into the market for five years, knew all the players, as they had been my customers. Many were friends and thought I had been treated badly. We traded, at least in part, on sympathy."

The company needed a name. They liked the name of the local Whitford Country Club and also joked they hoped to be successful enough to join the club one day.

"We were looking for a name that did not mean anything," Willis explained. "Ted and I were both young and still getting carded when we went out for a drink. We felt if we used our own names, people would feel the company was run by our fathers. If we were asked a tough question that we did not want to answer, we figured the questioner would ask what we thought our fathers would say. Since Whitford did not have any meaning, whatever we could make it mean was up to us. Through no fault of our own, it turned out to translate and be pretty pronounceable in most languages."

So by March 1965, they were in business as Whitford Chemical. They'd wanted to call the company Whitford Corporation, but the Pennsylvania secretary of state would not approve the use of that name.

"There was a Whitford Sales Company," Willis said, "which was an auction house, and the secretary of state thought there could be confusion between the businesses. Whitford Sales Company auctioned horses."

The two new entrepreneurs found a building—actually a two-car garage that had been a Firestone Tire Shop—near downtown West Chester, Pennsylvania. They painted, cut out a small corner for an office, put up a wall for a lab, hung a couple of doors, and bought the equipment they'd need.

Hiring was a function of people needing jobs, being willing to work hard, and accepting shares of stock in lieu of higher salaries. They hired a worker who knew what he was doing and a skilled technical person who had not been getting along at LNP.

Among the reasons the new partners chose to compete in the Teflon compounding part of LNP's business was that the capital needs were much lower than those of thermoplastics compounding. Also, the customers were established and easier to reach than in the much more diverse field of reinforced thermoplastics.

Their early products offered an improved, free-flowing molding compound, and they created some process improvements that benefited their customers. Their theory was that if LNP's business had grown and supported its employees, there was room for Whitford Chemical. That turned out to be the case. The new company—and its employees—managed to avoid starvation, and Whitford Chemical became profitable fairly quickly.

Right from the outset, they honed their competitive skills.

"We were a lot hungrier," Willis said. "The competition was overconfident. Our products were at least as good, some better and more uniform and, in most cases, our delivery was quicker. I had joined the Society of the Plastics Industry (SPI), the majority of whose members were customers or potential ones. And I was in their faces a lot. We convinced them that we wanted their business. About once a month, we did some direct mail that was not frivolous but had some humor to it. We talked up new products and provided samples."

Revising the Game Plan

At an SPI meeting in 1969, however, a quick head count showed more suppliers to the industry than customers of Whitford Chemical. In the four years Whitford Chemical had been in business, five new resin suppliers had entered the market to compete with DuPont, and all but one also sold filled compounds, thereby directly competing in Whitford Chemical's niche. It was not a reassuring situation. The major producers were each making a line of filled compounds, and some of Whitford's customers were even making their own. The potential market was shrinking.

Meanwhile, Whitford chemist Paul Fields had figured out a way to take a polytetrafluoroethylene (PTFE) micropowder with a very fine particle size, developed at Whitford Chemical, and put it into a binder resin to create a new coating. The result was easily ground to a fine, uniform particle size to produce a new product: Xylan 1010. (More on how this came about in chapter three.)

Willis and Rehmeyer decided that PTFE micropowders like Xylan offered a brighter future. In late 1969, they sold Whitford Chemical to Pennwalt Corporation, a producer of PTFE and the sole resin producer without a line of filled compounds. They retained the micropowders segment of the business, now under the corporate name of Whitford Corporation (this time approved by the Pennsylvania secretary of state). The new product line was high-temperature-capable, wear-and-corrosion-resistant coatings, which used the PTFE micropowders as the active material (see opening diagrams).

"One way of looking at the business is we do wet what we used to do dry," Willis explained. "There are plenty of differences, but the finished product has most of the same components as the dry blended products, just a different and much more complex avenue to get there. DuPont owned the coating business with the Teflon name and products. Pennwalt did not want to devote the time, energy, and especially the money to gain entry into the consumer market."

In the process of selling the filled PTFE compounding business to Pennwalt, Whitford agreed to take back the assets and equipment used to formulate and make PTFE coatings, formulation methods and equipment very different from the dry blending business. That amounted to about $60,000 in physical assets. The intellectual property was not valued and likely had no value. Willis and Rehmeyer had the money LNP had paid them when they were fired, the book value (in cash) of their LNP shares, plus the income from the Pennwalt sale.

"That kept us going for the first full year in 1970, along with the sales of $95,000," Willis said. "The second year brought sales of $149,000 in the US and $41,000 in the UK. Along with that came the ability to borrow money from the local banks: first $50,000, then $100,000 from a more friendly and knowledgeable banker when the first $50,000 was called on ten days' notice, despite the fact that we were current on all payments. It is no longer legal to make a call like that. The bank does not have to renew but cannot arbitrarily call a loan without a reason."

The Struggle to Find a Footing
Whitford struggled financially for the next several years, changing banks, selling some shares to two friends for $50,000, and some employees who also bought shares. The company's agents in Taiwan forgave $90,000 in commissions for a similar value in shares, eventually owning about 4.25 percent of the outstanding shares, currently valued at about $3.1 million.

Meanwhile, Willis pledged all his assets, including his home in Downingtown, Pennsylvania and the Pennwalt stock he had received in the sale, as well as some shares owned by his children. His father loaned the company $100,000 in the form of a debenture so that it could be pledged on the balance sheet as an asset. Upon his father's death in 1972, Willis inherited the debenture, and the pledge continued.

The sequence of events in 1969 and the years immediately following had a significant effect on forming Whitford's emerging corporate personality. In the aftermath of that SPI meeting, the company found itself confronting an ever-increasing pool of competitors in an aspect of Whitford's business that had helped establish the secure footing on which the company now stood. But Willis could also see that the room was growing overcrowded and the opportunities diminishing. Whitford had moved beyond the immediate challenges of just keeping a newly formed company running. Now Willis and his colleagues had an exciting new product to sell in Xylan 1010. They would go on offense, instead of pulling back into a prevent defense. The first score occurred quickly.

Willis was having breakfast at a diner with longtime friends from SPI and Xomox Corporation, a major producer of valves. The Xomox executive brought up a sticking problem his company was having with one of its products. Willis said Xylan 1010 might solve it. The Xomox exec said he was willing to try it and did. Xylan provided a tough, low-friction coating to withstand the constant wiping of a rubber seal on a valve actuator. At the same time, it was capable of being cured at temperatures sufficiently low to avoid heat distortion and outgassing of the aluminum casting of the actuator housing.

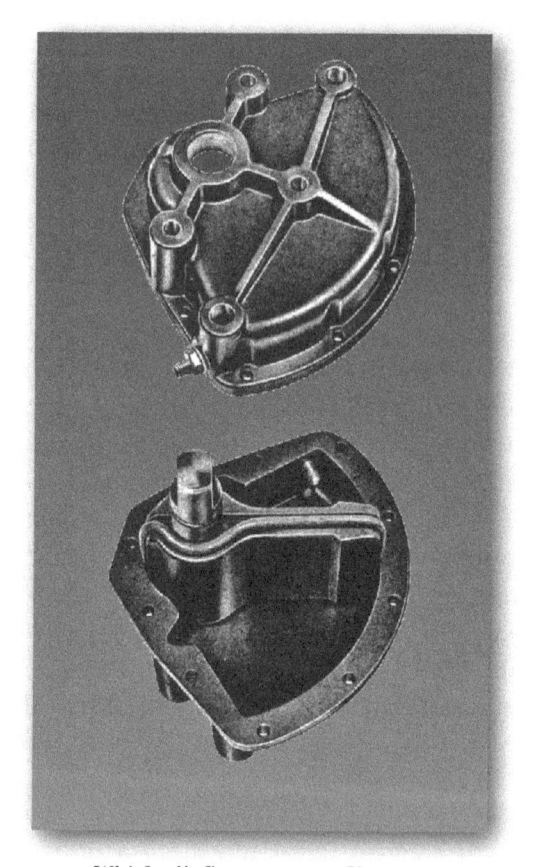

Whitford's first customer, Xomox,
with Xylan-coated valve actuator.

That year, Whitford sold a grand total of five gallons of Xylan 1010 to Xomox for use on its valve actuators. But what started with one small product application blossomed into thousands of applications for many companies, spanning more than four decades. Xylan 1010 set Whitford on the path of creating products to compete with the Goliaths of the high-performance coatings industry. To this day, it remains one of Whitford's most popular products.

Opening an Overseas Office

With a saleable product line now in place and new variations on the theme in development stages, it was time to establish an international presence. How that evolved began in the late 1960s. Ted Rehmeyer was working at Whitford part time while going to the Wharton School, where one of his classmates, John Powell, a British citizen, was working on his MBA. Powell had met an American woman at Penn and decided he did not want to go back to the United Kingdom for the summer, preferring to carry on his romance in the United States.

"Whitford was having some process problems that we needed to solve," Rehmeyer explained. "I mentioned it to John. We got together after class at the dining table at the Phi Gam house, across the street from Wharton. John scratched out, on a piece of paper, all of his ideas about how he could work through the problem."

It was toward the end of the spring semester, so Whitford hired Powell as a summer intern, and he worked out the problem.

"He came to work wearing his tweed jacket," Rehmeyer said, "which I thought was more appropriate for Scotland in the winter. He continued for the next three years as a summer employee, but when he finished school in 1970, even though it was a finance school, he didn't want to go back and work with numbers in London. He was a manufacturing type of guy."

However, Powell did want to return home with his new American bride and start a business. He recalled sitting in Rehmeyer's garden and musing about their futures. He was interested in continuing a relationship with the company but did not want to be part of what was then being called the "brain drain": some of the United Kingdom's best minds emigrating to the United States.

"Neither of us had said much," Powell explained, "but both had thought that Whitford Corporation could do the left hand of the Atlantic and, if I went home, my new operation would do the right."

He approached the partners about considering him to set up a Whitford in the United Kingdom. Thus, Whitford Plastics, Ltd. was born in 1970, in the unused bedroom of a half house in Sale, a suburb of Manchester. They chose the location principally because the city had the largest international airport outside London. Shortly thereafter, Powell moved the company to a thirty-two-hundred-square-foot industrial site in the "new town" of Runcorn, Cheshire.

"New towns were all the rage in England at the time," he said. "Public housing was also part of the master plan. So my wife and I moved with the new factory location. In effect, the ghetto previously located in Liverpool was moved across the Mersey River to new buildings. The location had the overwhelming virtue of being inexpensive. And the town council held the adjoining buildings for us. Over a period of twenty years, Whitford ended up occupying nearly twenty thousand square feet of contiguous space."

Confronting Tax, Duty, and Patent Issues
Challenges came at the fledgling operation immediately.

"First there was the 'import deposit scheme,'" Powell said. "Prime Minister Harold Wilson's government had decided, in its wisdom, that all importers must deposit fifty percent of the value of any importation with the government for six months."

The fee was an estimation of the taxes and duties that might apply but hadn't been calculated yet. Customs regulations and tax rates applicable to certain goods could change between the date the taxes and duties were estimated and date of import into the country. This was a problem, since Whitford United Kingdom's early supplies were to come in from the United States, and the UK operation was cash poor. Whitford's US and UK companies were both at that stage of development at which they consumed money.

Then there was the matter of the "exchange control."

"In the UK, my interest and the US interest were adding equity as needed," Powell explained, "while Ted and Dave were also trying to fund Whitford. But the exchange control required that any equity from me—and my rapidly depleting funds—had to be matched at the same time by an equal amount from outside the UK. Indeed, bank borrowing in pounds sterling had to be equally matched. Funds in the US were also rapidly depleting. At one point my American father-in-law provided us with a US dollar loan to overcome one of these cash crises."

At the time, Whitford's clear target was DuPont's TeflonS business. TeflonS was applied to things like saws, pruners, and various industrial components. The *S* stood for "stratification," which is what the coating did when cured. The fluoropolymer came to the surface to provide the needed low friction. But when the top surface had worn off, there was no lubrication left, making the product significantly inferior to Xylan 1010.

"Once we understood the key difference between Xylan 1010 and TeflonS, we started asking 'Why buy half a coating?'" Powell said. "The first key job we won was a coating for electric iron sole plates—the business side of an iron. Xylan worked, but TeflonS did not. The higher operating temperature of Xylan made the difference. Shortly thereafter, we secured Black and Decker UK (circular saw blades), Hoover UK (more electric iron sole plates) and James Neil (a major Sheffield maker of saws)."

These successes led straight into the next crisis: DuPont sued James Neil, Black and Decker, and Hoover for breach of a DuPont patent, which they said was infringed by the Whitford product these companies were using. The lawsuits gained widespread exposure with articles in the *Financial Times, Daily Telegraph*, and *Wall Street Journal*.

"Happily, we had taken out patent defense insurance," Powell said. "Even happier, our patent agent, who had advised that we did not infringe, had taken out his liability insurance with the same insurer. We could afford to fight this. Our customers' attitude was gratifyingly supportive. They let us fight the case. They did ask for indemnity, however, although they must have known that, from a firm like ours, it was worth little. One of them said they were not prepared to let their suppliers be oppressed. We got excellent, though expensive, legal advice. Eventually the process led to the point where DuPont was due to file papers in response to our latest submission. They did not do so. And that is how it stayed."

David had defeated Goliath. The pieces were now in place for the company to grow in the United States and abroad.

CHAPTER 3

XYLAN LAUNCHES A COMPANY

When you have competing theories that make exactly the same predictions, the simpler one is the better.
—OCCAM'S RAZOR

How often in the history of American business has a giant corporation ignored, downplayed, or simply rejected a business opportunity, while the tiny start-up saw the possibilities? How often has the recognition of that doable opportunity provided the start-up with the wherewithal to thrive? Welcome to Xylan 1010.

After the founding of Whitford Chemical in the mid-1960s, the company was a customer of DuPont, making Teflon molding compounds. Consequently, DuPont reps came calling, sometimes even bought lunch. At one of those sales lunches in late 1968, members of the DuPont coatings group were ballyhooing the introduction of TeflonS, which was a combination of a binder resin called polyamideimide (PAI) and Teflon FEP, a fluorinated ethylene propylene thermoplastic resin. The subject then turned to polytetrafluoroethylene (PTFE).

While listening to the DuPont sales pitch for TeflonS, Dave Willis was intrigued with the possibility that combining PTFE with PAI would result in a superior nonstick coating. He asked the DuPont people if they thought it could be done. Their no was emphatic. Making that happen would be a challenge, to say the least. Since PTFE had been discovered by a DuPont chemist in 1938, the company was the recognized authority on what could or couldn't be done with the product.

Complicating the ability to create the combination of PTFE with the binder resin was that PTFE was not stable in water. It would either gel or sink rapidly and therefore was virtually impossible to redisperse into a coating. Given PTFE's lack of stability in water, any experiments involving water would fail.

End of discussion?

Hardly.

An Idea That Wouldn't Go Away
Willis could not let go of the idea that if PTFE could be combined with a resin, which would permit it to bind to surfaces, it had the potential to become a much more attractive nonstick coating. Also driving Willis's interest in the possibilities of PTFE versus FEP resin combinations was the DuPont patent on the latter combination in TeflonS. At the heart of the TeflonS nonstick properties was the fact that the FEP would melt and stratify to the surface of the binder resin, thus creating nonstick properties at its surface. But when that surface began to wear, its nonstick properties began to wane. On the other hand, if a way could be found to disperse PTFE throughout a binder resin, it would be a much more saleable coating.

"Teflon is normally sold as a dry, white powder in twenty-five-micron to forty-four-micron particle sizes, mostly forty-four," Willis explained. "As sold, it is not a good powder lubricant. The particle size is too large and the molecular weight too high. It becomes useful when it is pressed into a desired shape and then free sintered (cured). Formed and sintered parts that do not meet the required dimensions, or are not suitable in some other way, can be reprocessed by chopping them into eighth-inch pellets and then grinding them into a twenty-five-micron powder, which can then be extruded into a tube or rod. The result suffers in physical strength but will work for many applications and is generally about half the price of the virgin resin."

Part of the process is to clean any contamination from the final product. This is generally done with acid and sometimes water. Irrespective of what is used, the product is wet at some time during the process and has to be dried, usually on trays in an oven at around five hundred degrees Fahrenheit. This drying also bleaches the gray product into a much lighter shade, nearly white, increasing the value of the outcome. However, the drying process also demands a high degree of caution because the powder can catch fire if the high temperature is applied too quickly. In fact, Willis's former employer LNP did have a fire in 1961, which turned the PTFE into a series of gray lumps. These lumps of partially over-sintered product were found to be good dry lubricants, however, when pulverized into powder form or used as additives to rubber, ink, and plastics. LNP sold increasing volumes of these materials over the succeeding years into those markets.

Later, when Whitford Chemical was formed, it too sold a competitive product into these same markets. The paint industry was a logical additional market, but certain chemical properties could not be overcome to solve the mixing and wettability problems that would create the coating Willis envisioned and vastly improve its sales prospects. So after the DuPont lunch, when Willis returned to the Whitford facility, he went to see chemist Paul Fields and explained the challenge to him. To research chemists, challenges are their stock in trade, especially if they are told something can't be done. Fields immediately began to consider what he would need to move forward. It was a near-dizzying array of requirements.

How Would DuPont Do It?

"I started to look at the way DuPont would look at this project," he explained. "It would have been expensive for them. They would have to commit people, a substantial budget, and a laboratory for doing it. So I'd need to set up a staff, do a tremendous amount of research, look into products that would be compatible with PTFE. Then I'd have to define the cost parameters. This would all take time. It would all take money. It would all be very complicated. The area that I had in our laboratory was maybe ten feet by twelve feet and ill-equipped. I'd have to make a release coating and a bearing surface that uses a fluoropolymer and can be applied at a low enough heat so it doesn't destroy the subsurface. That's where we were."

And, by the way, Fields was also in charge of doing the research concerning the other materials the company was working with at the time.

Despite his youth—he was in his early twenties at the time—Fields had some serious credentials as a chemist. Willis had become aware of his talents while Fields was in charge of research at a company called Mather Fluorotech, which bought resin from Whitford. When Fields was looking to leave Mather Fluorotech, one of his contacts at Whitford arranged a meeting with Dave Willis and Ted Rehmeyer. They liked what they heard and hired him.

Born in Corpus Christi, Texas, Fields was the son of a pipefitter who had worked on the Manhattan Project, which created the first atomic bomb. His parents had always instilled in him a curiosity and a will to explore new directions, which was characteristic of the approach he now brought to the PTFE challenge. He was convinced that the naysayers would not believe that a twenty-something guy shoehorned into a tiny laboratory at a company whose sales, when compared to DuPont's, wouldn't rise to the status of a rounding error could ever solve such a complex issue.

Any other questions?

Again, that's just the kind of challenge a research chemist could not let pass.

Occam's Razor

From the viewpoint articulated by the DuPont reps, the suggestion of mixing a Teflon PTFE micropowder with a thermoset resin to make a Teflon-like coating was not possible as simply a matter of chemistry. All the high-temperature resins viewed as necessary to allow for the combination were polar (as in what makes two magnets repel each other when the same poles approach each other). Similarly, the electrical charge on the polar resin repelled the same polar charge on the PTFE micropowder. In order to mix them, the charge on one or the other had to be changed or at least neutralized. And that was just one of the challenges Fields confronted.

"Many of the reasons that this could not be accomplished had solid technical validity, if you limited your thoughts to conventional processing of PTFE," Fields said. "But rather than making the problem more complicated, I changed my approach. I needed to move in a different direction. I went back to Occam's razor: "when you have competing theories that make exactly the same predictions, the simpler one is the better." So I looked at things that I knew. I'd been working with fluoropolymers for a long time and knew them very, very well. I knew their relationships with different chemicals."

Being intimately familiar with PTFE, Fields knew he had to do something about the chemical's long fiber chains, something he likened to having a box of springs.

"When you heat up the PTFE, the springs expand," he explained, "and when you cool it down, all the springs interlock and make a solid. If you put a bunch of the springs in water, they go to the bottom."

Letting Things Stew for a While
He had come to that point at which he had defined the major elements of his problem, so, "I put a whole bunch of things into my head and let things stew for a while." Stewing morphed into intense concentration.

"I have the ability to be extremely myopic," Fields said. "I push people away and can end up spending the night in the laboratory or spending days, one on top of the other, because time disappears when I am concentrating on something."

That Fields had drifted into a world of his own was not lost on his coworkers.

"I wondered if it was just sheer bloody-minded determination that would get Paul the result he wanted," said John Powell, who was also working in the lab at the time. "One morning when the building was unlocked, Paul was found asleep on the lab bench."

But Fields was homing in on a solution. At this point, Whitford was selling a dry PTFE powder called Whitcon, with a very fine particle size and controlled molecular weight, using a unique ionization process the company had negotiated via a licensing agreement. Putting radiation to the powder caused its molecular chain to scissor and made the PTFE links shorter. With the chain links shorter, the result could become useful.

Fields felt the answer to the polarity problem would be to marry the Whitcon powder to a resin used in magnet wire, but that would require the process withstanding significantly higher temperatures. Fields's solution was to "pre-wet" the PTFE with Freon 113, a high-boiling liquid fluorocarbon, then mixing the PTFE into that solvent until the low surface energy of the Freon 113 turned the PTFE into a heavy slurry. The slurry was then mixed with the carrier resin normally used as the coating for magnet wire. The mixture was stirred until the Freon was driven off by the heat generated. Then the PTFE and resin were mixed and remained in dispersion, contrary to what the experts from DuPont had said.

While this system accomplished what was needed to marry the disparate elements, problems remained. Freon 113 was expensive, and the process using it was finicky, needing careful supervision. But the end result was a coating capable of withstanding high temperatures while providing the lowest-friction and least expensive result: a fluoropolymer combination with outstanding adhesion to nearly every substrate surface to which it would be applied. TeflonS, DuPont's competitive product using FEP, was a more expensive fluoropolymer with the marked disadvantage of having a much lower working temperature. Over time, Fields found wetting agents—essentially soaps—that replaced the Freon 113 at substantial savings and ease of handling.

The Eureka Moment?

The successful combination of the two elements became Xylan 1010. Bingo! Time to celebrate?

"I'm not a very eureka-type person," Fields said. "I'm more like, OK, I solved that problem; what's next? If you want me to tell you I bounced around the room a bit, I'd be lying. I just felt 'hey, this looks pretty good.'"

At the time, criteria for naming a new product dictated using two syllables and very few letters; "Tef-lon," for example. A hunt through the dictionary produced "Xylan," a group of hemicelluloses found in plant cell walls and some algae. Five letters, two syllables, perfect. According to Fields, the start of the experiment was given the designation 1000, and he had solved the problem on his tenth experiment: ergo, Xylan 1010. The name and the numeric designation worked beautifully together.

The time window from when Fields was presented his challenge until he developed a successful result was just a few months. For all intents and purposes, it appeared that Fields had created the superior product for Whitford to take on the competition.

"At this point, the coating was in Dave's hands," Fields explained, "right where it belonged. I saw it as a technical challenge. But he saw it as a marketing opportunity."

In essence, the DuPont no at that fateful lunch in late 1968 had, inadvertently, given Whitford the opening it needed. With the development of Xylan 1010 and the company's future turning a bit rosier, Whitford established a dedication to new ideas and empowering people to explore and develop them. Over the years, the company continually spent a considerably higher percentage of its revenues on research and development than its competitors did. That approach has led to more than nine thousand different active formulae for coatings, while DuPont Chemours offers a small fraction of that number.

Mulling an answer as to why the DuPont representatives were so insistent that the problem he would face was not solvable, Fields reflected, "There are several things that were occurring during that time in the marketplace that could have been a catalyst for their vigorous effort to deter our research. The first was that, during the 1950s, DuPont's patent expired and 'Teflon' was becoming a generic name, much like 'Kleenex' and 'Nylon.'

Based on projections, there was sure to be a glut of product on the market. As new sources entered the marketplace, Whitford Corporation became a major consumer of the competition's resins. Also, I am guessing that, as one of the premier specialty coating manufacturers, DuPont would frown upon encouraging another potential competitor."

Understandable if one looks at the results the development of Xylan 1010 meant for Whitford. Having existed as Whitford Corporation for just the final two months of 1969, the company recorded only one five-gallon sale of Xylan 1010 for that year. But the product was so innovative, so effective in addressing the various coating markets, it has been a mainstay of the company's business to this day.

Moving On

Having played a pivotal role in setting up the original Whitford facility and creating the company's first and most successful product, Fields felt it was time to move on.

"To me, I'd accomplished what I was asked to do, and I never want to feel like I'm backing up to get my paycheck," he said.

Fields left Whitford after three years and went on to a variety of careers. He worked on the design for the Abrams tank, a mainstay of the US Army and Marine Corps, then worked on the cutting-edge technology of fuel cells. He taught hydraulics at the University of Delaware and started his own company. Further, "there hasn't been a space shot since the beginning that didn't have something I participated with or helped design," he said.

Recognizing talent is perhaps the most important element in building a new business. Dave Willis had put his faith in Paul Fields, and that faith was rewarded big time. Confidence in a colleague's ability often has the predicted beneficial effect on that colleague's self-esteem as well.

As Fields put it, Willis gave him "the self-confidence that has carried me my entire life. If you can truly touch somebody else, you can change the world. If you look at Whitford coatings, almost everyone has been touched by them, whether they know it or not."

Now a Baptist minister at a small-town church in Factoryville, Pennsylvania, and a counselor at nearby Keystone College, Fields is uniquely qualified to speak to the relationship between the metaphysical and the scientific.

"There are two kinds of scientists," he posited. "Those who want to disprove there is a God, and those who become scientists because they want to understand how He does things."

Postscript

After leaving Whitford to work on the Abrams tank, Fields designed a special seal for the tank. When the engineers began testing the seal, they found the tank was losing a lot of air. They concluded there must be a fault with the seal.

"There were literally dozens of engineers standing around not sure what the problem was," Fields recalled. "I said, 'You've got a hole in the tank someplace.' They said, 'No, we don't.' I said, 'I've done the math. That's the only answer. You've got a hole in the tank. It's as big as my thumb.'"

So Fields convinced three or four engineers and some technicians to climb all over the tank. Near the turret, they found the hole Fields had predicted. One of the engineers said, "No, it's a drain." So Fields stuck his thumb in it and said, "You've got a hole in your tank. You just renamed the hole and called it a drain, but it's still a hole."

Fields added with a chuckle, "That's kinda the way I do stuff."

Occam's razor lives on.

CHAPTER 4

THE EARLY YEARS BEGIN TO DEFINE A COMPANY

We were in the right place at the right time, and we brought science to a wildcat mentality.
—DAVE WILLIS

When Dave Willis and Ted Rehmeyer sold Whitford Chemical to Pennwalt Corporation on November 1, 1969, it was the most recent in a series of key decisions that were indicative of a corporate philosophy forming, even in these earliest stages in the company's development. Willis was very much attuned to the business landscape in which Whitford competed, and if it began to change, alter, expand, or contract, he wanted Whitford to be in step with what was occurring, even a step or two ahead.

Witness how Willis and Rehmeyer had launched a company after being let go by LNP, because they saw a business opportunity in Teflon compounding that had room for another player. Then, when DuPont presented its innovative new TeflonS coating, Willis was convinced there was a large market for such coatings. But with DuPont holding the patent on the combination of components used to make TeflonS, Whitford would need a viable alternative. Rather than just some basic variation on the theme, Willis felt Whitford could create a superior product, and the marketplace would react favorably. Thus, the development of Xylan 1010.

At the Society of the Plastics Industry meeting in 1969, where it became apparent that the compounding universe was overcrowding, Willis determined that Whitford would leave the compounding business, take its dynamic new product, and place its bet squarely on a future making PTFE micropowder–based coatings. These decisions took the pulse of the market and allowed Whitford to redefine itself and take advantage of changes in the industry.

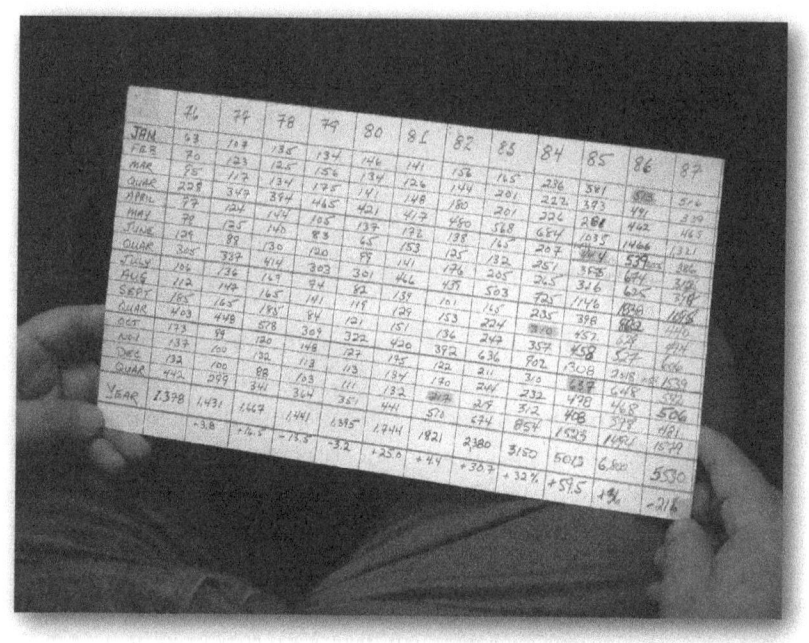

Whitford's "computer" before buying a Commodore 64.

With only two months of 1969 making up the new Whitford Corporation's "first year," Xylan 1010 sales totaled just $2,000 for that November and December. The next year dawned with the Whitford roster made up of just four employees in addition to the two principals (both unpaid): Paul Fields, the chemist; a one-person production department; a one-woman office "everything"; and a rep to split the sales territories with Willis. Willis also served as overall manager and Rehmeyer as part-time accountant. Sales grew to $95,000 for the company's first full year in 1970. Nonetheless, monthly sales figures were small enough for Willis to keep track of them on shirt cardboards from the dry cleaners, a practice he kept up until he got a computer in 1990.

How to Stay for More than Forty-Five Years
Finding the personnel to staff the initial bare-bones operation took some creative recruiting. Larry Leech, who became the one-man production department, wasn't even quite sure this was the kind of work for him.

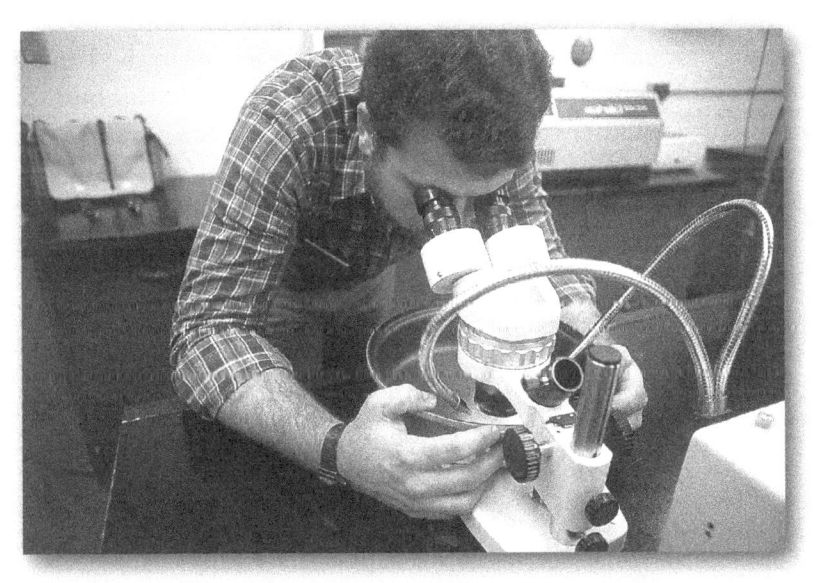

Larry Leech working on early developments.

"I was still in college at the time," Leech recalled, "majoring in chemistry. But I wasn't sure I wanted to stay in chemistry. So I applied for some jobs in the local chemical industry, one being Whitford, the other LNP, Dave's and Ted's previous employer. Both companies had a relatively long interview process, and I was getting desperate for money, so I took the job at Whitford because they made the quicker decision. I looked at Whitford as a way to spend a few months and decide whether I wanted to stay in the chemical business. I never expected to be at Whitford beyond a year or two, but the company changed so rapidly, every time I'd get frustrated and think I'd want to try someplace else, things would change and I'd think, 'Maybe I'll stick a while longer.'"

"A while longer" turned into quite a bit longer. Leech stayed with Whitford more than forty-five years. During that period, he managed the lab, was conscripted to solve a production crisis, returned to the lab as director, and did tech-service trips to customers in Asia—just some of the many hats he wore over the years. Late in his career, as consumer team leader in the lab, he mentored technicians, who were majoring in chemistry but not quite sure whether to stay in the field.

Except for the interview process, Leech saw nothing of Willis during the first several months of his tenure, the latter being on the road beating the bushes for customers.

Taking Xylan on the Road

"We felt we had a product to compete with TeflonS," Willis recalled. "As DuPont's recent introduction into the dry-film lubricant market, it was really the first well-thought-out entry in that market. We decided to offer a similar product to the same market as an alternative, but with uniformity from batch to batch.

What took us some time to realize was that we really had a better coating for a very competitive price."

Xylan offered almost 50 percent greater coverage (300 square feet versus 218 square feet) for the same price per gallon. The PTFE in Xylan gave the coating an additional one hundred degrees Fahrenheit in use temperature, as well as a lower coefficient of friction. Whitford offered Xylan in several colors, while DuPont sold only black and green coatings.

Previous products from other suppliers tended to be combinations of phenolic resins and some graphite or molybdenum disulphide. They were black, always dirty looking, and never very uniform.

Armed with the better product but minimal brand recognition, Willis and the company's other salesman, Ron Seitzinger, needed a game plan. DuPont had developed and published an approved-applicator list of Teflon coaters, compiled over some ten years. Because the applicators were licensed by DuPont, their corporate names and addresses were published in DuPont's literature. It listed one or two companies in each of the major areas of the country that specialized in applying its coatings. It was an obvious target list for Whitford.

Seitzinger, who had had a couple of bad experiences with air travel, would not fly, so he was given the northeastern United States as a sales territory—that is, as far as it made sense to drive. He soon landed Sun Plastics in Detroit as one of the company's first customers. (As an emphatic testimony to Xylan's staying power, Sun Plastics, now run by the grandson of the founder, remains one of Whitford's best customers more than forty years later.)

49

Willis took the rest of the country, with his efforts concentrated in Houston and the oil and gas industry. Some tragic explosions in the area, over the years, had created an opportunity for Whitford. A safety council had been established among the chemical factories along the Houston Ship Channel. The chairman was a representative of Union Carbide, which had suffered fatalities in one explosion. He soon became a believer in what Willis was telling him about Whitford's batch-to-batch uniformity, which was crucial to creating a coating that would permit consistency in properly torqueing the bolts on the flanges. As a result, virtually every user in the area was soon specifying Whitford, coating studs and nuts by the thousands, creating enough business to keep the company operating.

"We were in the right place at the right time," Willis explained, "and we brought science to a wildcat mentality."

Two Old Friends Reunite

While Dave Willis placed a heavy emphasis on sales, he also knew that he needed a coordinated, supportive marketing effort. Ironically, his commitment to the relationship between marketing and sales had cost him his job at Liquid Nitrogen Processing in the early '60s.

Although Willis knew that he needed to create a marketing effort for his new company, he would not have anything even close to the money he had spent at LNP. With sales of just $2,000 for Whitford Corporation's first two months of existence at the end of 1969 and sales slowly creeping upward in 1970, he would have just a few hundred dollars to commit instead of thousands. Nonetheless, Whitford needed to start creating an identity in the coatings business in general to carve out paths to additional prospects. In fact, the company needed to let potential customers know it even existed and what products it sold, especially when it intended to go up against competition that had been in the Fortune 500 for years.

As he traveled the country in those pre-Internet days, Willis looked in the local Yellow Pages to find coating applicators who claimed to use Teflon but who were not on the DuPont applicators list. Given the territory to cover and the limited personnel and resources with which to do that, the company needed to find a way to keep up with the list as it grew, while getting the word out to other applicators that Whitford existed. Willis knew there was someone who could help him do this or, at the very least, give him some sound advice. That led to a meeting with an old friend, Tony Weir, and the modest beginnings of the marketing effort that would play a major role in establishing Whitford's brand identity over decades.

Weir and Willis had been friends since they'd met at prep school and had maintained contact and their friendship over the years, despite having taken different paths in business. Willis knew that Weir held an impressive position as a creative director at Ogilvy & Mather in New York, and Willis needed to tap his brain on what to do. He called Weir. With the company barely a year into its existence, the two friends sat down to talk.

"Dave began by explaining his business," Weir recalled. "He described his products as 'slippery paint' and said he needed some sort of advertising to spread the word that Whitford existed and had something worthwhile to offer. I asked him what kind of advertising budget he had in mind, recognizing that it would not be as large as the multimillion-dollar budgets I was used to working with."

"About $150 to $200," Willis replied.

"You mean a day," Weir asked, "or a week?"

"No." Willis laughed. "That's the annual budget."

Undeterred, Weir countered, "What's the size of the audience you hope to reach?"

"Probably forty to forty-five people," Willis answered. "But it's growing."

Weir felt there was only one sensible answer: direct mail. A list of prospects that small would be easy to manage in-house, where Willis's secretary could assemble and address the mailings, and the cost would be minimal.

Stretching Dollars but Addressing Markets
Weir knew that the first step in building a brand identity was to attempt to define the kind of image Whitford ought to project or how the company should be perceived by its principal target markets. He determined that whatever corporate communications he created should mirror the dominant personality traits of his old friend: outspoken, challenging, even aggressive; factual, helpful hard facts instead of soft claims; clear, irreverent, bordering on cocky; but also a sense of humor, not taking himself too seriously.

He decided on a series of mailings, done over a period of time, far enough apart so that each new mailing refreshed the message Whitford wanted to deliver without becoming bothersome because of excessive frequency. Each envelope would contain some sort of gimmick, a "touchy-feely" that indicated something dimensional was inside, along with a legend on the outside that piqued the recipient's curiosity enough to open the envelope and see what it contained. The letters were short, punchy, and heavy on the puns.

An early example included a penny coated with Xylan. It began "Here's a little something for your thoughts—and we don't mean the penny. We mean the coating."

After briefly extolling Xylan's virtues—that it cures at low temperatures, has incredible adhesion and superlative wear resistance, and comes in a broad range of colors (including copper)—the mailing concluded with the pitch and the offer: "The varied (and superior) properties of Xylan lend themselves to limitless applications heretofore impossible with a fluoropolymer coating. Why not call and tell us your problems? We may already have the answers. If not, we'll look for them."

Then came the shameless pun: "Now look at the penny again. When you think about it, it makes sense…"

Just like the company, the letters were straightforward, competitive, uncomplicated, with a sense of humor. Regarding wear resistance, for example, the same letter urged recipients to "try carrying that penny around with you for a few years. The penny may depreciate. But the Xylan coating won't."

Whitford-coated Scrabble chips came with copy that read "Xylan can be used as a coating for wear applications on virtually any surface—with equally good performance. Take those two Xylan-coated wood chips. Rub them together. If the Xylan wears off within the next hundred years, we'll send you two more, absolutely free."

Another mailing included one- and two-cent stamps in a small plastic envelope, with copy that read "Both stamps cover the same area. But one does it for half the price...We know you've heard DuPont's side of the story. Now we want you to hear our two cents' worth."

It was direct-mail marketing that was clear, brief, informative, and clever, not to mention different from anything the recipients had seen. The letters assumed readers of wit and intelligence. It wasn't long before recipients were telling Whitford salespeople they not only read the letters but looked forward to receiving them.

Thus, having just those few hundred dollars to spend, but a highly targeted audience to address, Weir's solution was practical, its execution ingenious. His direct mailings stood out from daily junk mail and forced his audience to take notice, and he could send follow-up, equally clever mailings as money trickled in.

The Acid Test

What happens when you put something to the acid test? In most cases, that question is just a manner of speaking to make a point. But as Whitford began to grow and generated a bit more to spend on marketing, the company began to advertise in targeted media addressing its industrial clients.

Early Whitford ads dealt with the reality of an acid test on bolts and nuts sporting its coatings versus those treated with competitive coatings. The visuals also included the results of bromine, caustic, and salt-fog tests, all conducted by a third party at the behest of a producer of fasteners for the oil and gas industry. What the visuals showed was dramatic. In each case, the Whitford-coated bolts and nuts suffered only minimal to moderate damage, while the others suffered extensive damage to total failure, with nuts frozen to the bolts. In every case, the Whitford-coated nuts remained free to turn.

Weir also extended the shelf life of the ads, insuring maximum impact by using them as part of the direct-mail program.

"Enough said," extolled the Whitford direct-mail piece, which included a copy of the ad. "After all, one picture is worth 10,000 words."

A Different Operating Philosophy

It was not difficult to suspect that, as a large, publicly held enterprise with little or no competition, DuPont would have some weaknesses born of size and overconfidence. After all, the company had been the only game in town. For Whitford, with a handful of customers and few products, about the only things it could provide were better, more customized products and quicker delivery times. This meant listening carefully to what potential customers said and understanding their problems, creating specific solutions to those problems, and getting product out the door as soon as possible—going far beyond the service normally expected.

Customers willing to discuss their problems, each of which was often a little different from the others, found attentive listeners at Whitford. And that attentiveness to those little differences began to steer Whitford in a direction that eventually became a formal—and important—part of its operating philosophy.

While many companies develop products in the abstract and then try to bend customer needs to fit those products, this often leads to a group of products that are packaged and sold off the shelf. Whitford, on the other hand, began to grow along with the requests of various customers who wanted slightly different coatings, customized to give them greater corrosion protection, better durability, or more release. In some cases, even all three.

Whitford's Xylan 1010 already had solved a specific problem for the Xomox Corporation: a coating that could withstand the constant wiping of a rubber seal on a valve actuator. (See chapter two.) Taking the Xomox solution as an operating model, the next step was to expand its market potential to a growing list of potential customers. The most obvious prospects were those companies on the DuPont licensed applicators list, a group of about fifty skilled coaters scattered around the United States and Canada. It was an excellent starting point for personal sales calls, supported by the direct-mail program.

Customizing to Meet Customer Needs

Whitford setting its sights on breaking into the business of fluoropolymer coatings became a classic case of a David confronting Goliath. Not only was DuPont infinitely larger, it had deep pockets (Whitford's were virtually empty), vast research budgets (Whitford had no such budget), extensive sales and marketing departments (Whitford had neither), and a history going back to the beginning of the nineteenth century (Whitford Corporation was a newborn).

What were the principal challenges to overcome if Whitford could hope to compete? Two stood out: the consumer market—cookware—was clearly "owned" by the DuPont Teflon name, products, and marketing muscle. Less obvious but equally clear to Whitford's technical people: Xylan, as it was initially formulated, was not a cookware coating and would not stand up to the rigors of stovetop conditions. (Although that later proved to be a rush to judgment and turned out not to be the case.)

Based on those early conclusions, the only markets open to Whitford were the industrial applicators that needed the unique combination of properties that Xylan 1010 offered. While these customers were smaller and more diverse, the unit prices were higher; the profits greater; and perhaps most important, these niches were so small they were of little interest to DuPont.

As companies in the industrial markets producing nuts and bolts and other, equally prosaic items learned about the benefits of release coatings, this additional market appeared among applicators that provided such coatings. While close to the traditional Teflon market, those in it did not want to pay for the privilege of using the brand name. Whitford was able to supply materials for such applications without running head on into the Teflon brand. Over time, these inroads into the market became substantial for Whitford yet were still insignificant enough not to attract DuPont as a competitor.

Xylan 1010's advantages were obvious: greater coverage, a more flexible cure schedule, better adhesion, higher and lower use temperatures. DuPont's competitive product had to be cured at a much higher temperature than Xylan 1010—high enough to do damage to some metal substrates, such as tool steels and

57

aluminum castings. This became an important selling point for Xylan.

During Whitford sales calls, applicators asked many questions concerning the product: color, gloss, coverage, ease of use etc. Among the properties that applicators wanted were a number of challenges that Whitford had not yet addressed.

The most useful comments involved what applicators viewed as 1010's disadvantages concerning their specific needs. For example, Xylan had a matte finish that marred when rubbed. Not good for many uses. In response, Whitford developed Xylan 1014, a version that contained less PTFE for a more attractive finish, while maintaining all but very long-term wear resistance. Another comment led to Xylan 1006, a version with more PTFE for applications that needed greater release.

Other requests were for a product that would withstand the high pressure that PTFE resins did not. The answer was Xylan 1052, a coating that added molybdenum disulphide, which is an excellent high-pressure lubricant. To make that product visibly different, Whitford added a yellow pigment, which produced an attractive, deep green. It turned out that the pigment was also a superb lubricant, so 1052 ended up with three synergistic lubricants: the PTFE, molybdenum disulphide, and the cadmium pigment. Whitford later removed the cadmium, kept the 1052 number, and moved the cadmium to a product called 1053. All but Xylan 1052 and 1053 were offered in a variety of colors. (Molybdenum disulphide is an intense black and difficult to color.)

Applicators who coated products for the oil and gas industry wanted better corrosion resistance, which was accomplished with the addition of a special corrosion-resistant pigment and named

Xylan 1070. The pigment was a lead-chromate compound that worked well but, because of the lead, soon became unacceptable from a safety standpoint. Whitford replaced it with other, more acceptable compounds that resisted corrosion.

Customer Service Pays Dividends

Within its first full year in business, Whitford had a half-dozen customized products for highly specific and quite diverse uses. Sales were climbing. Meanwhile, DuPont continued to offer only a few products under the TeflonS name and only in black and green. Also, DuPont offered very little technical information with its products. Whitford seized on this failing to create literature with helpful information that could be given to customers and that they in turn could offer to their customers. As a result, Whitford became the go-to supplier for a growing list of industrial applicators.

As an ongoing response to the DuPont name and influence, emphasis on customer service continued to rise in importance at Whitford, with more sales calls, more contacts via direct mail, and more helpful technical information, all of it increasing the company's visibility and positive perception among customers.

Developing multiple materials formulated to serve specific functions for specific customers became both necessary and desirable. Whitford's desire to solve a customer's problem via customization rather than simply selling a product off the shelf made life more complex and more difficult for the competition. This, of course, meant investing in the development of many different formulae.

Whitford's business model began to succeed, and business started to expand. In addition to the Houston "Oil Patch,"

Chicago became an important market, as did the industrial regions around Rochester and Buffalo in upstate New York, with applications for automotive and photocopier components. Additionally, Whitford picked up coaters in the Los Angeles area.

Expanding Overseas

Meanwhile, prospects in Europe began to display opportunities to expand the business there. Whitford Plastics, Ltd. (WPL), had been established by John Powell in the United Kingdom in 1970 (see chapter two), and Chris Copeman, who joined as co-partner roughly six months later. WPL's business makeup paralleled that of the US Whitford company. On the other hand, Powell felt that the industrial market potential was much greater in Germany than in the United Kingdom. At that time, to do any amount of business in a continental country, a company had to have a presence in the form of a legal entity. Consequently, Powell moved his family to a tiny town north of Frankfurt and established Whitford GmbH. Once Whitford established entities in the Netherlands, Spain, and Switzerland, Copeman had his work cut out for him as salesman for the European area.

In 1984, Whitford moved into Hong Kong, then Brazil in 1986. Although the expansions were viewed as risky at the time, Whitford chose to follow its customers as they left the United States for other countries, with each of these locations having some real basis for new business. Whitford offices were one- and two-person operations until the early '90s, when Whitford merged its European business with its business in the United States to become Whitford Worldwide Company.

"Worldwide was a bit of an overstatement at the time," Willis allowed.

Hardly the case as the company moved into the twenty-first century. In early 2006, Whitford Worldwide opened its eighth manufacturing facility, this one at Jiangmen in China's Pearl River Delta. The manufacturing sector in the Pearl River Delta plays a significant role in Jiangmen's economy. Chief among its industries are the manufacturing of household appliances, motorcycles, stainless-steel products, and textiles, all potential markets for Whitford.

Whitford Ltd. moves to the Pearl River Delta in Jiangmen, China.

Among the chief attractions for locating a manufacturing facility here are the four international airports within a sixty-mile radius, a port just three miles away, and just a two-and-a-half-hour ferry ride between Jiangmen and Hong Kong. More than one hundred of the world's top corporations have offices in the Jiangmen Industrial Park.

Of the new facility's sixty-five thousand square feet, thirty-nine thousand were dedicated to production and warehousing, expecting to turn out seventy-five hundred tons of product during its first year. The facility also included significant space for future development.

Today, in addition to the United States, Whitford has manufacturing facilities and/or sales and marketing offices in Brazil, Canada, China, Colombia, France, Germany, Hong Kong, India, Italy, Japan, Mexico, Singapore, Spain, Turkey, the United Kingdom, and Vietnam.

Since the creation of Whitford Worldwide, the company's sales have had near-continuous year-over-year increases, save for the occasional hiccup, usually the result of short-lived downturns in the general economy.

The Business Model Continues to Develop

If there was a modus operandi emerging during these first two decades of Whitford's development, it was staying on top of the ever-changing needs of individual members in an increasingly diverse roster of customers, then responding accordingly. Doing that could be as basic as paying close attention to what customers needed and addressing those particular needs with specific solutions. It could be a matter of following customer migrations, even to distant locations around the world. These were often emerging markets, which the competition was not focused on or had little interest in serving until Whitford had already established its firm foothold. It could be a matter of persistence in convincing a customer of the merits of a Whitford product that would meet that customer's needs at a competitive price, even if the customer initially had difficulty seeing that its problem begged for a uniquely Whitford solution.

In the simplest of terms, Whitford had made it nearly a religion to stay close to its customers in good times and bad—an operating philosophy that would serve it well and result in dramatic growth during the years ahead.

CHAPTER 5

HOW TO SURVIVE A MELTDOWN

The test of a great manager is getting out of big trouble.
—CHRISTOPHER ANNAS, FOUNDER
AND CEO, MERIDIAN BANK

Concentration during Whitford's early years was on industrial business, since the company had no coatings for cookware and could not challenge the popularity of the Teflon name in the consumer marketplace. Within a few years, however, Whitford was presented a business opportunity among potential customers who wanted coatings that were easy to clean but did not require the Teflon name to support their saleability. Early examples included base plates for Mr. Coffee appliances and parts for National Presto's Fry Daddy and Burger Maker.

Mr. Coffee, whose spokesman was Yankee baseball great Joe DiMaggio, had become very popular. A key feature was the warmer plate, which required cleaning and was an ideal application for a nonbranded, nonstick coating such as one Whitford offered.

Meanwhile, Presto had introduced family-size deep-fat fryers, which allowed consumers to make their own French fries or deep fry chicken parts. Those fryers also had become very popular, and executives at Presto, like those at Mr. Coffee, felt no need to brand the nonstick coating used.

Whitford was able to supply FDA-compliant materials for these applications without running head on into the Teflon brand. Over time, inroads into these markets became substantial for Whitford, yet they were still insignificant enough not to attract DuPont as a competitor. In fact, nearly forty years later, DuPont still does not offer serious products for these applications. Continuing discoveries of such niche applications provided the wherewithal Whitford needed for survival in the early years.

In the early 1970s, Whitford saw another sales opportunity in cookware at chain stores, which advertised low-priced offerings (today euphemistically called "opening price point" or OPP products). Whitford developed a coating for chains such as Dollar General and Family Dollar, again using Phillips's PPS resin, which was capable of withstanding the temperatures associated with cooking and baking. Combining the resin with PTFE created a coating that worked well for inexpensive cookware.

Given the volume of cookware sold in those chains, that part of Whitford's business grew to the point where Ted Rehmeyer could come on board full time. Rehmeyer concentrated his efforts in Asia, where the principal segment of manufacturing for that cookware was located. Even at that early stage in the company's development, Asia had already become a key area for the company's growth.

By 1977 and '78, coatings for these products had grown to represent almost 40 percent of Whitford's business, which had reached about $1.5 million in sales. Prospects for continued growth in this area were good, and the company's business was now reasonably well balanced between consumer and industrial customers.

The Phillips Melt-Flow Meltdown

Then Phillips Petroleum changed the melt flow of the Ryton PPS resin it was supplying to Whitford from greater than five thousand to less than fifty on the same scale, significantly reducing the polymer's ease of flow. Whitford was not informed of the change. In fact, Phillips denied making any change to the melt flow. Nonetheless, the difference resulted in Whitford's customers not getting a smooth, glossy finish on their products. The new coating also required more surface prep. The failure of the prep procedures, which had been working prior to the change in the resin, became apparent when containers filled with cookware were arriving from Asia with the coatings sitting loosely atop the cookware.

However, even if inadequate prep were a factor in the failure of the coatings, "good materials would not have been as sensitive to their surface prep variations," explained Whitford's Larry Leech.

The inability to make a product that satisfied 40 percent of its customers caused Whitford to lose that business within just four months of the melt-flow change. Before the problem with the Phillips resin, Meyer Manufacturing of Hong Kong was Whitford's largest customer. That business disappeared completely. Consequently, overall sales dropped below the $1.5 million mark established in 1978. The sudden loss of 40 percent of the business was not just a reduction in profits; it threatened the existence of the entire company. Head count was reduced from twenty-eight to eighteen, a regrettable necessity in order to save the company and the jobs of those who served Whitford's remaining customers.

"We needed money to last more than a couple of weeks," Dave Willis said. "Everything I had was pledged. My only possible source of an asset was from my Aunt Betty, who lived in Phoenix. I made a visit, and she loaned me her only asset: $110,000 in Wyeth stock. I pledged it and was able to get enough money to survive for a few months, albeit on a much smaller scale."

Although business began to rebound, and most of the money crises became bumps instead of mountains, the pressure became too much for Ted Rehmeyer.

"His education was as an accountant," Dave Willis said. "He had become a CPA after college and before joining LNP and then Whitford. The constant lack of funds fell on his shoulders and made the pressure too great for him. He also pointed out that the company was in no position, nor likely to achieve one, that would support two bosses. In November 1978, he took a job with Meyer Manufacturing, selling its cookware products in the United States. He later moved on to his own company, making and selling cookware specifically designed for use in microwave ovens."

Barbara Ficca Hayward, who had been the partners' executive assistant, took over the money management. While walking into such a disastrous circumstance could have been intimidating for Hayward, she saw it as a demonstration of confidence in her abilities.

During the Phillips crisis, "empowering" required using all the ingenuity Hayward could muster to juggle the company's finances.

Some weeks there was not enough money to meet payroll. When she issued the weekly paychecks, if there was a smiley face on the envelope, employees could cash the check. If not, they would have to call the next week to find out if the check was good.

She also had to juggle cash to pay suppliers.

Barbara Ficca Hayward with other senior managers (L-R) Chris Copeman, Dave Willis, John Powell and Tony Weir.

"When I couldn't pay them," Hayward explained, "I would call the suppliers and tell them, 'I promised I would have a check out to you tomorrow. I don't have the money. Allow me to make the promise again for next week.' They always agreed, and I always kept my promises."

To gain more breathing space, Whitford sued Phillips. The suit went nowhere in the early months until it came to the attention of Phillips's senior counsel, who invited Willis to Houston to have a discussion. He recognized what Phillips had done was illegal, since no change of materials or manufacture is permitted under law without advising the customer.

The settlement was an agreement to supply the "old resin and manufacturing technique." The value from Whitford's perspective was to obtain about $300,000 worth of resin at no charge. Whitford's auditor allowed the company to put the resin in inventory and on its balance sheet at the undiscounted value, in essence giving the company its value as an asset, effectively a profit of $300,000. Whitford was then able to get the money to have Aunt Betty's Wyeth stock released.

A Banker's Invaluable Assistance
Cash flow, of course, is the lifeblood of any business, and the role of a banker can be key. Helping determine Whitford's future fell to a young banker named Christopher Annas with Industrial Valley Bank (IVB), at Whitford's branch in West Chester, Pennsylvania.

"Whitford was an existing customer when I inherited the account," Annas explained. "As a junior commercial lender, I was pretty excited to take over a complex, international company as a customer."

That excitement soon bumped up against reality when Annas was called upon to help with the crisis caused by the Phillips problem.

"From a banker's perspective, this severely diminished our collateral because the inventory was bad," he said. "The accounts receivable were not being paid because of the faulty product. Dave Willis was in crisis mode to save the company. He gave the bank all of his personal assets to support the loan."

"Our business was so shaky that I had a permanent appointment with Chris each week to review our orders, sales, and receivables," Willis said. "He was very encouraging, which we certainly needed. I am not sure how far up the chain he sent the information, but our loan was never called or threatened."

It helped that the bank's operating philosophy was to do all it could to help a client survive rather than pick at the bones after it died.

"IVB management was somewhat unique in that they tended to stick with customers longer than most banks would during troubled times," Annas explained. "We used many senior managers in our credit administration to help devise a plan for Whitford's borrowings during the crisis. Dave worked with the bank personnel in a positive and constructive way during the crisis, which served him very well, and there was a great deal of trust built. Dave got latitude in areas where others might not have."

How two parties work together to deal with a crisis successfully tends to create lasting business relationships.

"The relationship moved along very nicely after the crisis," Annas explained. "It's unusual because once a company gets in the dungeon of a bank, it usually doesn't get out. It's a testimony to how Dave handled himself during this time that the relationship really blossomed afterward. This included expanded credit and a closer relationship with Dave and senior management at the bank."

The association of business and bank continued to expand long after the Phillips crisis subsided, and Whitford went from defense to all-out offense.

"Dave is an aggressive businessperson and saw great opportunities as a David against DuPont's Goliath," Annas said. "He expanded plants both domestically and overseas, which required loans for equipment and inventory. IVB accommodated Dave in all aspects. As a rookie loan officer, I was the beneficiary of Dave's business acumen and really enjoyed hearing his vision for where Whitford could go. I was a big advocate for Dave and Whitford and used this advocacy to convince the bank to support the expansion."

How Did the Situation Spin Out of Control?

Could this problem be laid solely at the feet of Phillips Petroleum and that company's irresponsible decision to drastically alter the melt flow of its product without alerting its customers? Or was it a Whitford issue, the failure to continually test raw material to ensure it was up to spec? Was Dave Willis getting any sleep at night, knowing that the company he had nurtured into an early success was teetering on the brink of collapse and that all his personal assets would go down with it?

The melt-flow issue was surely a setback—a major setback—but Willis knew he had marketable products. Whitford would have to find a solution to the raw-material issue. The company would need to reestablish the viability of the product by coming at the problem from a different direction. Willis was confident his people would find the wherewithal to overcome this setback. After all, Paul Fields had created the coating DuPont said could not be done and had done it not that long ago. Whitford would just have to figure some way to pay the bills, get a positive revenue stream going, and hang on until a solution to the chemical problem could be worked out, product could meet customer expectations, and the whole cash-flow process was in place once again.

The Phillips resin problem was one of chemistry, albeit not a problem of Whitford's making. Nonetheless, chemistry was Whitford's stock in trade. Chemistry, therefore, would have to lead to a solution.

"Once we realized what was going on, we checked with our UK facility to see if any of their customers were complaining about the same issue," Larry Leech explained. "Most of their customers were industrial, not consumer, and they were not seeing the same sensitivity, even though they were using raw material with the same lot numbers as we were. So we brought in the UK base technology, which was product ground in ball mills using other surfactants, and that resolved the problem from the standpoint of adhesion. However, we never had a product that looked as good as the product we had before the Phillips problem."

An unexpectedly beneficial outcome of the melt-flow crisis was the company recognizing the need to expand its client base. While struggling with the losses in the cookware-coating business, Whitford was building a more diverse line of products. The company had added a coating containing molybdenum disulphide: Xylan 1052. It added a series of silicone polyester products—1514 in white—sold to Clairol for its Crazy Curl hairstyling wand. That coating later morphed into 8514, sold to the bakeware market in a variety of pewter and black metallics. Sales of these products were quite small, however, when compared to the loss of the cookware business.

How to Survive a Recession

While the company's US business level stayed below $2 million until 1983, Whitford's products had good margins by industrial standards, affording it the ability to continue to build its product line, call on customers, and make limited expansion of the field sales force on a regional basis. From 1983 to 1987, company business had more than tripled to $6.8 million. But factors beyond a company's control hovered in the shadows until they could gain enough energy to cause mayhem.

On Monday, October 19, 1987, stock markets around the world crashed, shedding a great deal of value in a very short time. The crash began in Hong Kong and spread west to Europe, hitting the United States after other markets had already declined by significant margins. The Dow Jones Industrial Average fell 508 points to 1,738.74, or 22.61 percent in one day. Whitford's business dropped a commensurate 24 percent. Once again, the company went into crisis mode.

"We instituted graduated pay cuts," Willis explained. "The more money you made, the larger the percentage of the cut. This made more sense than layoffs, which then would create a need to train new people when the business came back, which it did the next year. At that point, the previous pay levels were put back in place and the differences repaid over time. The pay cuts became what amounted to a 'free loan' to the company in our time of stress."

By 1991, Whitford's US business topped $10 million for the first time.

More than two decades after losing the Meyer Manufacturing business during the Phillips crisis, Whitford won it back. Once again, DuPont played a role, albeit unintentionally. During the economic downturn, DuPont instituted a no-fly ban to save money. As a result, Whitford became the tech-service representative at Meyer, since DuPont would not let its own employees visit the customer. By that time, Meyer had relocated to Thailand and had become the second-largest cookware producer in the world. It took twenty-three years of calling on the customer to get the business back, but that perseverance paid off in the end.

While some conventional wisdom may define the best managers as those with spotless records of achievement, Chris Annas, now CEO of Meridian Bank, offered a different take.

"I always tell them that the test of a great manager is getting out of big trouble and rebounding to be a great company," Annas explained. "Dave Willis has done that. Eventually, he worked his way through the Phillips problem, and Whitford survived. To this day, I use Dave Willis as my prime example of a great manager."

CHAPTER 6

How to Keep It Going

> *You miss one hundred percent of the shots you don't take.*
> —Hockey great Wayne Gretzky

By the onset of the '90s, Whitford had left survival mode behind, had established its viability, and could now exhale collectively, perhaps even settle into a comfort zone. The company had come to life modestly a full twenty-five years before but, over that quarter century, had managed to grow its business with innovative new products it sold to targeted markets. It had proven its mettle, toughing out a near meltdown and weathering a global market crash on a grand scale. Whitford Worldwide sales, which topped $10 million for the first time in 1986, had doubled by the early '90s. All indications were that growth was likely to sustain itself at comfortable levels into the foreseeable future, given the solid foundations the company had built with its existing customers. But any sense that the company would settle easily into a comfort zone defied Whitford's history. Whitford's senior management would only be satisfied with continued, even accelerating, growth, in effect the antithesis of satisfaction. Since its inception, Whitford had never done well with "satisfied."

"We have never gotten comfortable with our success," Dave Willis said. "That is, we do not take it for granted, and we never feel as though we have finally arrived, finally solved all our problems, finally can coast. When it comes to innovation, there is always the next great formula or product or application. We spend a lot of money on R&D because we are curious, and we are never satisfied. It's the kind of mind-set that has carried us through good times and bad. We just never let up."

When *In Search of Excellence*, the ragingly successful business bestseller by Thomas J. Peters and Robert H. Waterman, debuted in the early '80s, the authors listed their number one attribute for a successful business as "a bias for action." This was an attribute that, by that time in Whitford's history, had already developed into a corporate mantra.

Nonetheless, in the David versus Goliath contests with DuPont, Whitford had to pick its fights, generally tactical forays into smaller markets. Systematically, Whitford identified targets, then its salespeople were persistent at attacking those targets, convinced that the superiority of the company's product line, along with its competitive price structure, would win out, provided customers and prospects were apprised of such competitive advantages on a regular basis. Even if a prospect wasn't ready to buy early on, once exposed to the advantages of the Whitford product line, those attributes played like a leitmotif beneath the louder music coming at the prospect from the bigger competitor. The factor or factors that could push a customer into Whitford's corner varied. In the case of Macy's, it began as a pricing issue.

Gaining a Foothold at Macy's

Taking on DuPont at Macy's would not seem like the kind of big fight the little dog could hope to win. Then again, sometimes the big dog itself creates the opportunity.

Early in her career, Fran Attilio Groesbeck was the youngest product manager in Macy's housewares department. One day, a representative from DuPont walked into her office and informed her that because Macy's was using DuPont's SilverStone logo on its private-label cookware line, DuPont was going to charge an additional 8 percent for its use. That did not sit well with Groesbeck. Shortly before her encounter with the DuPont rep, however, Groesbeck had met John Badner, then Whitford's director of marketing, at the huge International Home and Housewares Show in Chicago. She decided they needed to talk and gave him a call. Badner came to see her, and they went over her requirements and various Whitford coating options.

"We had very strict testing in Macy's product development," Groesbeck explained. "When we got pans with Whitford's Quantum2 coating, we ran all our tests, and the results were great. When we got quotes, they were coming in much lower than the DuPont product. We were stunned. So we did a little negotiating and some final tweaking."

Fran Groesbeck with John Badner.

Since Groesbeck and her colleagues at Macy's didn't really know Whitford that well, and having just been burned by DuPont, they felt it would be best to use their private-label name on the nonstick cookware so they could change the coating again at any time and not have any issues. Whitford had no problem with that.

"John Badner even helped us come up with the name and the design of the logo: 'Tools of the Trade Nonstick,'" she explained. "The sales were fantastic, and we didn't see any increase in returns."

In effect, Whitford became Macy's partner, and together they developed Tools of the Trade Premium Nonstick, then launched two gourmet-level cookware lines with Whitford's Excalibur coating. Whitford even designed and provided labels for this Macy's product.

"It blew away the competition," Groesbeck said. "Pricewise, we were significantly lower. We also made a stainless-steel line and a hard-anodized line. We hit price points we could not have hit otherwise. It was a phenomenal partnership, and I never looked back. With everything I did involving nonstick, my first call was to John Badner."

As she began to work more with Whitford, she noticed that she never got a no from the company. Instead, she heard answers like "We'll give it a try" or "We'll take a look." Even if "no" turned out to be the ultimate answer, because an idea did not work or a coating did not match the need, it was always preceded by a concerted effort to deliver.

After Groesbeck left Macy's for a position with a private product-development company, she said DuPont offered Macy's a big chunk of money to reclaim the business, and Macy's took that for a couple of years.

"The problem is," Groesbeck said, "with that big chunk of money, you don't get any support or questions answered or help with product development. You *need* to have a partner. For example, when you buy Farberware, there is a big company called Meyer behind it. You get all kinds of QC and advertising support. When you have a private label, you do it all yourself as a product manager. So every component needs to have a partner. Whitford eventually got the business back, and Macy's still uses Whitford coatings today."

Crazy Curl Hair Curlers
During the early '70s, Whitford was unearthing more and more opportunities to work with companies whose products would gain little, if anything, from paying extra to use a proprietary

DuPont product name. Sometimes an opportunity presents itself when you have the right person in the right place at the right time. Clairol presented just such an opportunity, and Whitford had the man on the spot to take advantage of it.

First consumer application of Xylan. One of Whitford's first ads.

Ted Rehmeyer had been in England on vacation with his family, but he also wanted to get a firsthand look at the business there, begun by his former classmate and now business colleague, John Powell. (See chapter two.) Meanwhile, back in the United States, Whitford got a call from executives at Clairol, who wanted someone from the company to go to Clairol's factory in Kalundborg, Denmark, and discuss hair-curling wands.

Rehmeyer was conscripted to interrupt his vacation and get a flight from London to Copenhagen, where he rented a car and drove to Kalundborg, a little town sixty miles away. Clairol executives, he was told, wanted to make a new and different kind of curling wand.

"For centuries, ladies had been sticking irons in fires, then curling their hair with them," Rehmeyer said. "Witness the many photos of the marcelled, dramatically wavy hair women wore during the Jazz Age. They were doing some serious hair curling with superhot tongs. Since Clairol was already synonymous with hair products, someone at the company had come up with a much more user-friendly device that held some water, got hot, then was able to spray more water to help hold the curl."

The problem was that the chemicals women used to wash their hair left some residue and were acid-based. That acid attacked the metal in wands. A protective coating had to be put on the metal, but it couldn't be sticky, had to be able to withstand high temperatures, had to resist the acidic residue after hair was washed, and had to have some release characteristics so it didn't rip hair out. Given the market potential in succeeding with such a coating, Whitford lab technicians in the United States went to work immediately.

"Dave Willis spent a lot of time in the lab," Rehmeyer recalled. "Staff from senior management to lab and production personnel got to work mixing raw materials together in various inventive ways, until they came up with a coating that worked. The result produced a substantial piece of business."

Clairol's Crazy Curl became a huge success. Farah Fawcett, one of Hollywood's biggest stars at the time and famous in part for her bountiful, beautiful, blond hair, became spokeswoman for Clairol's ad campaign. The wands became one of the first recognizable appliances in the consumer market to carry a Whitford coating.

The George Foreman Grill

Having identified opportunities on the consumer side of the coatings business, especially among cookware companies that did not want to pay extra to use the Teflon name, Whitford began to doggedly pursue this business. The center of that world was in Asia, and it was growing by leaps and bounds.

In the 1970s, Ferro Corporation, headquartered in Cleveland, Ohio, with offices throughout Asia and subagents in other major countries, became the agent for Whitford's line of coatings. Over the next ten years, Whitford was building a business in cookware products in Asia, albeit slowly. By the early '80s, however, it had become clear that Ferro was not representing Whitford very energetically. Fixing the problem required Dave Willis's personal attention.

Michael and Richard Lee of Multitop with Dave Willis.

"I started to travel to Hong Kong on a Friday, arriving on Saturday evening," Willis explained. "I would take Sunday to recover, make calls on Monday, Tuesday and Wednesday morning, then fly to Kaohsiung on Taiwan's southern coast."

When Willis got to Taiwan, he would meet up with Richard Lee, Ferro's subagent there. They would travel together, making sales calls, eventually working their way to Taipei, Taiwan's capital, on Friday night. Sometimes, if time permitted, they would make calls Saturday morning before Willis would head for Tokyo to catch the Pan Am flight back to the United States.

During these business trips, Willis had become so impressed with Lee that he hired Multitop, Lee's company, to be Whitford's direct agent in Taiwan. By that time, Multitop had established several offices in China and captured most of the wok and small-appliance business there. But those victories were just a warm-up for the really big score—the George Foreman Grill—and Whitford was involved with that one from the very beginning.

The evolution of the grill began modestly. The product was originally launched as the Steak Grill by Toastmaster, an independent company later acquired by Salton Corporation. (Salton was growing its small-appliance business through acquisitions.) The grill was to be manufactured by TK China, maker of most of Salton's small products and a coater that had been using Whitford coatings since the company's founding in Taiwan. Willis and Lee had already been calling on TK China, whose founder, T. K. Wu, was considered a manufacturing genius. What separated the Salton grill from others was the grill plate, which was slanted so the fat would run into a tray, getting rid of most of the liquid.

With the product starting to sell, Salton felt the need to promote it on a grand scale. To do that, however, would require a spokesperson with an established identity. Whomever was chosen would need to be relevant to the key sales point of the grill: the healthier outcome associated with the removal of the fat. George Foreman's talent agency was sure it represented the perfect client for the job. They got in touch with Salton and negotiated a deal for him. Foreman already had a well-established identity as an Olympic gold medalist and two-time world heavyweight boxing champion. Also, a key determinant was the fact that Foreman loved to tell interviewers that he ate two hamburgers before each fight.

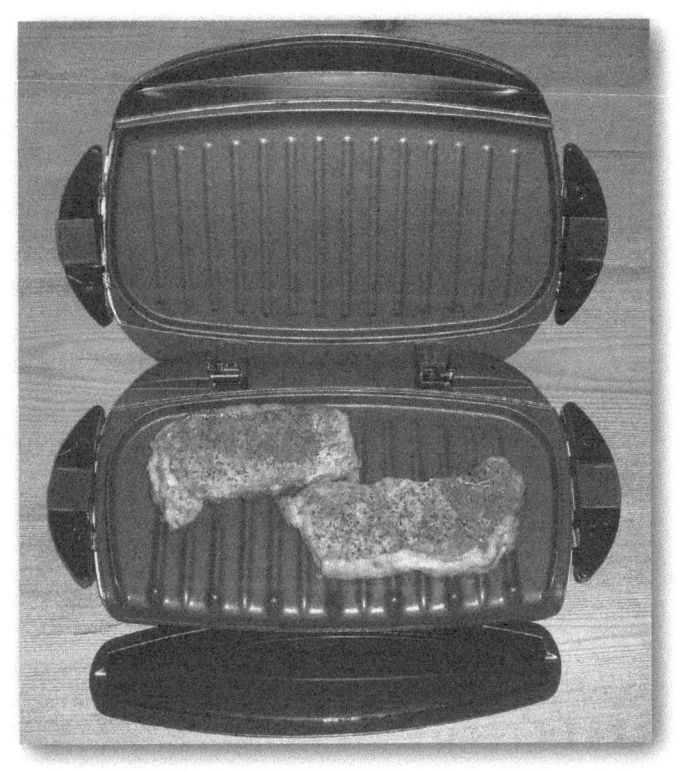

More than 100-million George Foreman Grills
were sold over a fifteen-year period

Foreman became the spokesman for the grill after regaining the world boxing title in 1994, at the age of forty-five. His cheerful personality helped make the grill an instant success. Consumers were urged to "knock out the fat" and "start eating and cooking healthier with George Foreman."

While Foreman's original contract called for him to be paid 45 percent of the gross profit on each grill sold, amounting to some $4.5 million a month in payouts, his deal was renegotiated in 1999 to a onetime payout of $137 million to use Foreman's name in perpetuity. It has been estimated that he made more than $200 million from the grill endorsements, far more than he ever earned as a boxer.

Nobody had seen anything quite like it before. Foreman became known as King of the Grill, and the grill was tagged the Lean Mean Fat-Reducing Grilling Machine, one of the most famous of all branded products and one that specified Whitford coatings.

More than one hundred million grills were sold over fifteen years. The grill, in its various incarnations, generated $400 million at wholesale at its peak in 2004.

"It trailed off after that," Willis said, "but we had about eighty percent of the business for years. We still do a fair amount."

The grill continues to sell throughout the world. In Asia, it is endorsed and promoted by both Foreman and movie star/martial artist Jackie Chan.

That the relationship built by Dave Willis and Richard Lee during those early '80s sales calls was mutually rewarding can be seen in the numbers Lee's company enjoyed.

"In 1983, Richard's sales totaled $30,000 for the year," Willis explained. "When he retired twenty-five years later, his company was doing $60,000 a day."

Selling in the "Oil Patch"

Scoring with Macy's allowed Whitford to add a universally recognized, big consumer products name to its list of clients. And best-selling products like Clairol's Crazy Curl wands and the George Foreman Grill had their own high-profile identities. Selling to the energy industry, however, involved addressing very specific requirements for companies whose components would operate far below the surface of the earth in very demanding environments—companies with virtually no high-profile identities. But addressing requirements for those companies and turning them into highly profitable relationships involved classic Whitford specification selling.

"The process starts with a company having an issue," explained Brian Willis, in charge of inside sales at Whitford. Prior to taking on that position, Willis had spent much of his career selling to customers in oil and gas industries while based in Houston. "An example would be dealing with wear caused by adhesion between sliding surfaces of a safety valve component. To address this issue, we coat a sample part with Xylan, either at Whitford's lab or using a local custom coater. Whitford may supply the coating sample free of charge. If the sample performs well, Xylan coating will get specified. After solving hundreds of these sorts of issues in the oil and gas industry, we now have hundreds of specifications for Xylan coatings."

Success with companies in the Oil Patch creates multiplier effects on a number of levels. As the companies grow, they tend to use existing Xylan specifications for new applications. Also, when engineers move on to positions with different companies, they tend to bring their Xylan knowledge with them and write new specifications for their new employers.

"We also offer to help engineers write the specifications for Xylan," Brian Willis said. "All these special efforts have snowballed into huge business opportunities for Whitford."

Such connections with clients in the Oil Patch, literally living among them, has had staying power. Over the years, Willis cultivated relationships with key accounts, got Whitford specified at the large original equipment manufacturers, and created lasting connections the company still enjoys.

While the Oil Patch has always been good for Whitford and has helped the company stay afloat when other markets have suffered, business analysts who follow the oil industry know that its history involves boom-and-bust cycles that can be very dramatic. Witness the very highs and very lows of the first two decades of the twenty-first century. Whitford coatings, however, are not captives of any one aspect of the energy sector. The company's coatings are ideal for the renewable energy industry as well, a rapidly emerging growth market.

"Wind, wave, and solar energy collectors also suffer from corrosion and weathering," Brian Willis said. "Xylan coatings play a major role in mitigating these issues."

Innovation and Consistency
If the aforementioned success stories resulted largely from Whitford's ability to provide innovative solutions to customers' needs, keeping that business has been a matter of supplying the consistent, top-quality coatings customers have come to depend on, batch after batch, year after year. The difficult lesson learned with the loss of Meyer Manufacturing's business, resulting from the Phillips melt-flow change, was that a company could never become complacent about the consistent quality of its product, given the many factors that go into its creation. In the case of the Phillips resin, expecting the supplier to continue to provide material consistent with Whitford's specs turned out to be an

erroneous assumption. (See chapter five.) While Whitford was understandably proud of the company's reputation for innovation, its emphasis on the consistency of its products was every bit as important, a major selling point for the company's sales staff. It was not just a matter of quality control of the product going out the door, but also assuring the quality of the raw material coming in.

Innovation carries with it the risk involved in departing from consistent, proven winners—witness Ford's huge gamble on a major redesign of its top-selling F-150 truck. In Whitford's case, however, heading down new paths is often driven by a customer's need for a yet-to-be-created coating. Such a product-development model then is a matter of "in addition to" as opposed to "instead of." The result of this Whitford-customer relationship has been thousands of unique formulae, which have greatly expanded Whitford's product line. On the other hand, Whitford is not averse to working without a safety net if the potential reward is worth the risk.

The company's venture into medical coatings involved substantial risk, including a seven-figure investment in the facility and equipment and hiring skilled professionals in a discipline new to the company. But with real risk comes the potential for real reward. Whitford's first shipments in July 2015 were about $7,000 worth of product. In August sales were up to $70,000, then in September they reached $170,000. (More on medical coatings in chapter eleven.)

Over its corporate history, forward motion has become ingrained in the company's approach to challenges. Continual challenges that demand ongoing innovation can create a level of excitement at the prospect of discovering Whitford's next great formula or product or application. The sense that the company's future would never be simply a matter of cranking out more and more of the products already developed was established literally at the outset. If indeed this commitment to forward motion had its beginning in chemist Paul Fields's creation of Whitford's first coating after the DuPont people said it couldn't be done, Fields's response to his success—"OK, I solved that problem; what's next?"—also set the company on its course toward its thousands of formulae for legions of clients all over the world.

CHAPTER 7

Modern-Day Alchemy…But This Time It Works

I tell a supplier's new sales rep, "Put the brochures back in your car, then tell me what you've got in the development pipeline."
—Kurt Mecray, Whitford USA technical director

Dr. Leonard Harvey, Whitford Worldwide's technical director, placed a small, clear plastic container on the desk before him. It contained a viscous, yellowish liquid. The look on Dr. Harvey's face was almost boyish.

"I made this yesterday afternoon in the lab," he said. "It's a solution of a polymer we didn't know if we could dissolve or not. Using our solvent technology program, we were able to. This product has a forty-degree-higher heat tolerance than what is out there in the market right now. You are seeing something right at the very beginning. It'll take maybe six months to a year to generate products out of this, but this is a big step."

How Whitford is able to innovate so effectively is via what Dr. Harvey called "platform technologies." One such platform involves solvents. Employing data from previous experiments in that technology, he managed to create the new polymeric solution.

"If you want to be successful in the scientific discovery area, it's not just happenstance," he said. "You've got to set yourself up for success. If you want to create good products, you've got to set up these base technologies, which we leverage into products. We can combine them to create new products, which have features of each of our platforms, to form the superior technologies that we have right now. We have a whole storehouse of things in the pipeline."

Not surprisingly, Dr. Harvey came to his intense interest in chemistry early in life. Born in Liverpool in the United Kingdom, he went to University College Cardiff, then on to a PhD at the University of Liverpool, winning the faculty prize for his doctoral work. After university, he joined British Nuclear Fuels and was assigned to a group called "special projects."

"You should never be in a group called 'special projects,' if you can avoid it," he said with a laugh. "You are doing things no one else can or wants to do. At BNF, if you weren't a mathematician, physicist, or an engineer, you were beneath contempt. They considered chemists almost the unwashed."

Nonetheless, he became completely absorbed in his work.

"I was working on explosions and playing with some really big toys," he said. "I was only in my mid-twenties and had a huge research budget, because money was no object. At one point, I bought all the helium in the northwest of England, took it to a site, and blew it up a stack in fifteen minutes to see if it would vent the building via a Venturi effect. It worked."

After five years, however, he began to lose interest and decided when that happens, you move quickly. He took a number of other scientific positions, one of which involved relocating to the United States, where he eventually attracted the attention of Dave Willis.

"It was 2002," explained Mike Miller, who was Whitford's worldwide technical director at the time. "Dave got a resume from Leonard Harvey, showed it to me, and asked, 'What do you think?' I said, 'There's only one job for him—mine. Give him my job, and find something else for me.' Dave said, 'OK, we'll make you chief operating officer.' Len and I fit together very well. Leonard was more into research than I ever was. I was always more hands-on."

While Dr. Harvey immediately respected Willis's corporate leadership, he was equally impressed with his grasp of the technology.

"Whitford is a technology-driven company," he said. "Dave is a technophile, which is one of the reasons I have enjoyed working for him. He is very knowledgeable in that area. You would be foolish to underestimate his ability to comprehend the technology."

Emphasis on Innovation

Dr. Harvey found he fit well with Whitford's near disregard for conventional wisdom, its disdain for "can't-do."

"I describe myself as being full on all the time," he said. "I like to work hard and play hard. I try to cram as much into my day as I reasonably can. I'm a very positive person. I am given a lot of latitude, so I use my creative side much more than I would in other environments. One of my professors once said, 'You have a refreshingly unorthodox approach to subjects.' I don't tend to look at things in a conventional way, which can be a problem sometimes, but it can be an asset as well."

Whitford's emphasis on innovation—and consequently, its larger research and development budgets—also fit well with Dr. Harvey's full-on attitude.

"We get a great deal more money than we normally would for R&D," he said. "Certainly more than our competitors. That's great for me, but it's also a double-edged sword, because when you are given that much resource, you need to deliver. And deliver well."

Over time, delivering has involved an intimate understanding of fluoropolymers, enhancing that understanding via continuous experimentation, then applying the knowledge derived to product design.

Fluoropolymers have very low surface energy, which means other liquids tend to bead up on them rather than spread out over the surface of a nonstick coating. A drop of cold water, for example, beads up on a nonstick coating because the drop has higher surface energy. Hot water has lower surface energy, and soapy water even less, which is why it gets underneath foodstuffs and helps remove them from dishes. The low surface energy provides the release. In scientific terms, cold water has a surface tension of approximately seventy-two dynes per square centimeter, hot water about fifty-six, soapy water about forty. PTFE, the nonstick fluoropolymer, is only about twenty-one.

How Does a Nonstick Stick?

So then, how does a nonstick coating stick to the surface of a pan to which it is applied? It's a function of the coating, along with special adhesive additives, spread out over the surface of the pan, achieving an intimate bond with the surface when the coating is cured at high temperatures. The adhesion process is improved by roughening the surface of the pan, which creates tiny peaks for the coating to grab onto when cured.

An important aspect of creating Whitford's innovative coatings begins with the raw materials produced by its suppliers. Kurt Mecray, Whitford USA's technical director, focuses on identifying materials that have the potential to adapt to Whitford's innovative approach to product development.

"A lot of what we do and the materials we use were never intended to be used in the ways in which Whitford uses them," Mecray explained. "That is our expertise: taking materials with unique properties and getting them into a form to allow for the production of liquid coatings. A lot of the engineering resins that we use as binders were developed with certain industries and certain applications in mind, never considering that we at Whitford might get our hands on them and start producing liquid coatings with them."

How to find out which raw materials may be suitable for Whitford's purposes becomes a matter of experience in knowing what to look for.

"We do it," Mecray explained, "through monitoring various publications, trade journals, information retrieval services that track the activity of suppliers, what's being talked about in academia, monitoring patents, and so on."

How Whitford manages to ferret out those specific raw materials that can be manipulated into its coatings is a matter of knowing how to recognize what will work for the company, even if a supplier is unaware of the use Whitford could make of it. While sales reps who have a history with Whitford understand the unusual attributes the company is seeking, new reps following a canned presentation on a sales call may be completely blindsided.

"Often, one of the first mistakes a new salesperson for one of our suppliers makes is bringing in a bunch of brochures on paint-related raw materials," Mecray said. "I tell the rep, 'Put the brochures back in your car, then tell me what you've got in the development pipeline. What do you see as advantageous with that material, and can I play with it?' It's not out of the question that we take a material that's not even commercial yet, play with it, and provide feedback to the supplier about what looks interesting for us, which then steers their development activities. It can be a good give-and-take relationship. I'm very willing to be a guinea pig to test new materials, because that gives us the advantage of being first to market."

If Whitford is able to work with a raw material that is pre-commercialization, by the time the supplier is fully commercial and its reps are pounding the pavement to the competition, Whitford may well have a two- or three-year head start to market with a product that is new and unusual.

Mecray is particularly suited to this role. He holds a degree in material sciences from Penn State University, and his association with Whitford goes way back, literally to his childhood.

"My family were neighbors with Dave's, so he watched me grow up," Mecray said. "Dave was very forthcoming in offering me an opportunity, which I took. Whitford has been my only employment since college. I've been here since 1989."

Beginning with a Challenge

Combining raw materials into a coating to address a customer's specific needs often begins with a challenge.

"As an example, let's take a customer who needs to coat a valve in a system pumping water with hydrochloric acid at two hundred degrees Celsius," explained John Russo, Whitford USA's lab manager. "We begin attacking the problem with a resin resistant to HCL and able to withstand the two hundred degrees Celsius, then alter the level of the fluoropolymer at various percentages. Next, keeping the fluoropolymer level constant, we alter the percentage of the resin. We employ this kind of ladder study of ingredients in various volume relationships until we hit the performance specifications we need. But since we have so many formulae, we first look to see if we have what is needed among them, and, if so, we are good to go. A lot of this is tribal knowledge, a benefit of being here a long time and knowing if we have a standard product that is going to do what's needed."

Russo sees the balance that Whitford has struck between solving the immediate needs of current customers and the longer-term investment in R&D for new technologies as critical to the company's longevity.

"We need to be working on products that will be going into commercialization in two plus years ahead," he said, "but the trick is doing that while also sustaining the current business and keeping the customers well serviced with today's products."

That twofold objective was the reason that, years ago, Whitford divided its lab into what it designated Tech Service and R&D. The company thereby assigned people to service the immediate needs of customers without having to take others from their work on development. The move allowed the development chemists to stay focused on just that: development.

"When we talk with our customers, generally one of the first comments they make is that they appreciate the special attention they get from Whitford," Russo explained. "Meanwhile, we are expending a large amount of resources on research and development to keep those customers happy with the products we create that they'll use years into the future."

The Excalibur Coating System

One of the ongoing challenges of nonstick coatings has been how to extend their lifespan when they are subjected to the wear and tear of frequent use. Rough treatment such as scratching, cutting, or abrading can chip and loosen a coating from its substrate. That in turn reduces the coating's nonstick surface area and the corrosion resistance of the item that was coated.

Reformulating coating chemistry to suit specific uses is one approach to the problem of longevity. Whitford's "different paths" thinking, however, produced yet one more innovative solution: Excalibur. Whitford promotional material labeled Excalibur "the toughest, longest-lasting, most durable nonstick coating in the world." The company had the test results to back up this boast—Excalibur lasted more than one hundred times longer than the competition in the punishing ball penetration test.

With Excalibur, Whitford created a "system," not simply a new coating. It is applied during a unique, four-step process. First, a stainless-steel substrate is abraded to roughen the surface. Next, molten, white-hot particles of stainless steel are sprayed onto it. The particles cool, harden, and become welded to the surface in a series of tiny peaks and valleys. Fluoropolymer is then applied, settling into the valleys and atop the peaks, bonding the coating firmly in place. Materials scraped across the surface of Excalibur skip along the peaks, unable to dislodge the fluoropolymer in the valleys.

Excalibur is used on all manner of surfaces from industrial to consumer products, manufacturing machinery to cookware, cutlery to plowshares. Since the process of applying Excalibur involves a series of customized steps, Whitford has compiled a list of coaters who have the expertise and equipment to do so.

Whitford-Learned Chemistry

John Russo sampling a coating.

Lab manager John Russo is a classic example of longevity, tribal knowledge, and the company's promoting from within. His grasp of chemistry is principally Whitford learned, with the addition of night classes and seminars. Just out of high school, he responded to a Whitford newspaper ad looking for production help.

"I didn't get the job," he said. "They picked someone else. Two weeks later, I got a call from Whitford and was told the guy they hired didn't work out and was I still interested. I said sure. I started in production, when there were just three of us. Shortly thereafter, they recruited me into the lab. Since then, I've done almost every job there: quality control, then running QC, shipping, production manager, finally settling into the lab, originally as a technician, then as technical services supervisor, now as lab manager. My job as lab manager is not on the technical side; it's running the lab. I have people working for me who do the technical work, and they're all degreed chemists."

Russo has been with the company more than thirty years. Then again, Whitford has had a tendency to create non-college-educated chemists, with perhaps no greater example than Tracy Jones.

Tracy Jones retired after forty years;
"a most rewarding experience."

"I had worked for a plumber," Jones said, "then for a trailer manufacturer as a spray painter. They laid me off in 1978. I took a job with Whitford, temporarily I thought, until the other job called me back."

Jones was hired in production to mix paint. After two years, when he finally realized he was not going to be called back to his previous employment, he decided to settle in for a while. However, he became another example of Whitford as a talent incubator.

"Dave Willis saw my potential," he said. "He pulled me out of production and put me into QC, then from there into the laboratory. I've learned the chemical side of the business from the ground up. Being here so long, you know how to tackle a project. It's just like baking a cake. Once you have the recipe, you modify it here and there. Over the years, I've been on the consumer, industrial, and textile sides. The challenges always get my juices flowing."

A Lab Refit

Over a fifty-year history, a chemical company's lab will undergo many transformations in equipment and procedures, and often longtime veterans can be resistant to change. By the late '80s, Dave Willis felt the Whitford lab was in need of refitting and updating. He went looking for the right person to handle the job. He found that person in Mike Miller.

The Elverson Development Lab.

Miller had started his career in 1964 with DuPont's Teflon group, where he worked for some of the originators of Teflon patents. In 1983, when DuPont sold its industrial finishes business to a company called Whittaker, Miller went to work for Whittaker out of a facility in New Jersey. He eventually became the lab manager of that division. But he was never happy with the nearly two-hour commute from his home in Pennsylvania, so he sent his resume around to colleagues and associates. One of the resumes made its way to Dave Willis.

"In 1988, I got a call from Dave," Miller recalled. "He said, 'I'm not a stock or bond salesman, so don't hang up the phone. I have a resume here of yours, and I need a lab manager. Would you be willing to come over and talk about it?' Whitford was fifteen minutes from my home."

In addition to the innate attractiveness of the short commute, Miller was impressed with what he found. But at the same time, he recognized there were deficiencies, especially in equipment, and the downside to the uniquely "Whitford expertise" of the lab personnel.

"They were worth their weight in gold to Whitford because they had such a background of the company's information," he said. "They'd been there a while, knew the products inside and out, knew what went into them. However, they wouldn't have been worth anything to another coatings company. They didn't have the knowledge of what it would take to put together a paint from scratch."

Miller also found the lab personnel's method of recording their experiments very disorganized. He felt he needed to bring order to the operation, and that would even involve some of the vocabulary. For example, while most referred to Whitford's products as "coatings," Miller said otherwise.

"Paint is what we make," he explained. "A combination of fluoropolymers, pigments, and a binding material that causes them to stick together and stick to something else. When you apply the paint, you produce a coating, a layer on top of something else. So it is our customers who make the coatings because they put the paint onto something."

Imposing a New Kind of Order
Miller set about transforming procedures.

"I initiated things like how to keep a notebook," he explained, "how to document the work you are doing, how to assign product codes, how to keep track of them. And as we grew and added more locations, those things became more and more important."

He admits to struggling with the specifics of the Whitford products' learning curve early on, but with his growing understanding came a growing level of confidence in his implementing what needed to be done.

"It was nerve-racking for a while," he said. "I didn't have the answers at my fingertips. I considered myself a reasonably good paint chemist. I had been brought up with some of the old timers at DuPont, who taught you the basics. But I didn't know the Whitford products, and they are distinctly different from any other kind of paint because they don't use ordinary materials. I knew fluoropolymers but did not have a background in PTFE and the other things they were using. Solving the problems in the lab put a lot of pressure on me in my first couple of years at Whitford. I was nervous. I didn't know whether I would be sticking around or not."

Initially, he had a hard time prying information out of people. As the new guy, he felt that lab personnel were husbanding the information or flat out didn't know what was appropriate to tell him. But ever the kind of person who can look at an obstacle course and figure out a way through it, Miller educated himself in a uniquely suitable fashion.

"I learned the business by writing faxes," he explained. "We'd get faxes from overseas about products, particularly from our only other active lab in the UK, but also a lot of agents in Asia. As lab manager, I would corral the guys who had the answers, and the administrative office would send out my responding faxes.

Eventually, I learned the business, and a trust developed with Dave and the people I worked with."

He began to create and install basic test methods. Issues as basic as crosshatch testing, which determines a coating's adhesion to a given substrate, were formalized in writing, along with some one hundred other test methods, most with subsets within a given method. The new methodology was so effective that when the Cookware Manufacturers Association (CMA) was developing engineering standards, the organization adopted the Whitford test methods virtually across the board.

Miller also took on an ever-increasing role in the operations side of the business. He provided substantial discipline, teaching the lab technicians and assistants proper development techniques, from ladder studies to more formal design of experiments.

"Whitford took many very important steps forward, both technically and operationally, as a result of the contributions Mike was making," Willis explained.

Miller was chief operating officer until he retired in 2012… or sort of retired. Despite a big retirement party on a warm weekend in July, including a variation on the "So Long, Farewell" song from *The Sound of Music*, there was Miller back at his desk the following Monday, a turnabout referred to by staffers who had attended the weekend shindig as "a real waste of a good retirement party." He has continued as a consultant for the company on operations and technical issues. Among other accomplishments, he created a training session in how to make Whitford's unique paint and took it to Whitford manufacturing locations around the world.

Modern-Day Alchemy?

An unintended consequence of Whitford's genius for innovation was competitors knocking off the company's formulae with the inadvertent aid of the patent process.

Created ostensibly to protect proprietary results like those emanating from Whitford R&D, patents, as public documents, nonetheless have been used by unscrupulous competitors to shortcut the entire R&D process and go to manufacture with products virtually indistinguishable from Whitford's. Ironically, such piracy has driven Whitford to be ever more innovative.

"So many of our products were being copied," Dave Willis explained, "that I decided the only way we could keep ahead of them was if we made truly unique products: in other words, things that couldn't be knocked off. It's very hard to reverse engineer these formulas."

Offense as a defense: ever the Whitford way.

While the origin of the word "chemistry" has been debated for centuries, the most widely accepted explanation is that it derives from ancient Arabic or Greek variations on "alchemy." That word, over the years, has become most associated with medieval attempts to somehow magically turn base metals into gold. Chemistry is also a widely used metaphor for things that work well together. One's first reaction to watching water bead up and roll around like mercury in a fry pan with Whitford's Eterna coating could indeed create a feeling of seeing the results of some modern-day alchemy. On the other hand, the process that created the coating was clearly the most innovative kind of chemistry, so much of it involving materials that are not supposed to fit well together. The people who do the chemistry in the lab, those who put it together in the factory, then those who sell it to customers around the world...well, they definitely fit the metaphor of working together to make good things happen.

If Whitford's original chemist, Paul Fields, somehow managed the alchemy of turning a Dave Willis idea into the reality of a best-selling product, the chemists who have come after Fields have succeeded in keeping that winning streak going for more than half a century. It is really not much of a stretch to claim that Whitford's own brand of alchemy involves turning base materials into economic gold.

CHAPTER 8

Silent Partners on the Road

> *You have a grand gift for silence, Watson. It makes you quite invaluable as a companion.*
> —Sir Arthur Conan Doyle, The Complete Sherlock Holmes

The roar of takeoffs and landings above your suburban home. The loud conversations at your favorite restaurant. The drone of mowers, blowers, chainsaws, and wood-chippers. The inconsiderately loud cell-phone chatterers on your daily commuter train. Noise. Annoyance. The two words even have the same etymology.

Modern life seems to have diminishing refuges from the noise of daily routines. One of the few dependably quiet zones is the interior of your car, where the whisper of your tires against the roadway is the only counterpoint to the music of that state-of-the-art sound system the salesman pushed on you as an upgrade. In fact, "quiet ride" was one of the principal selling points that convinced you to buy.

So how did a car ride become insulated from the sound of the once-ubiquitous road noise, still evident in the city scenes of those classic black-and-white movies filmed decades ago? When did the engine noise turn to a quiet hum? Where does Whitford fit into these improvements?

Whitford products help many applications on any vehicle. The company divides its automotive business into two categories:

Flexible finishes: products that go onto weather strips and rubberized components (i.e., flexible substrates)

Automotive metal: the antifriction components—steering shaft splines, brake parts, solenoid valves, transmissions, compressor pistons in the air-conditioning system, nuts and bolts, and others

Over the past quarter century, automotive companies have made major improvements in the seals on doors and windows. They are wider, with a larger surface area, and are softer so they can produce a better seal. Initially, the rubber seals on vehicle doors were notorious for sticking in both heat and cold. At the time, the solution was to make the rubber harder, but that made the seals noisier. If the rubber was softened, the seals stuck.

"That seal in your car by your left ear goes back and forth and could do this itch-and-squeak thing," explained John Russo, Whitford's USA lab manager. "This was a big deal to automakers."

Whitford state-of-the-art sound lab.

    If quieter seals are a big deal to automakers, making them happen becomes a big deal for a coating manufacturer like Whitford. To ensure Whitford was on the cutting edge of new technology in this area, the world's most advanced noise-analysis technology equipment was installed as part of the company's move into its new headquarters and manufacturing facility in Elverson, Pennsylvania, in 2006. The ultimate objective was to eliminate the noise generated by the smallest of movements between surfaces such as car doors and their sealing systems. To minimize the impact of its surroundings, the sound lab is isolated from the building in which it is housed and "floats" on seven feet of fine sand. It is one of the most advanced such labs in the United States for dealing with noise, vibration, and harshness control of automotive weather stripping and is capable of measuring background noise with weighted decibel values at very low readings. The equipment is designed to replicate that "itch and squeak" of car seals.

"The answer is coating these surfaces with a nonstick or low-friction type of coating," explained Kurt Mecray, Whitford USA's technical director. "It helps preserve the sealing material, reduces the friction, which can cause squeaks and noise, and eliminates the sticking problem. All of this, of course, is invisible to the consumer. There is no reason for him or her to know the seals on a car door are coated; however, consumers have made that happen because they demanded that auto manufacturers make cars quieter."

Whitford Purchases Alpha Coatings

Turning state-of-the-art R&D into practical applications, however, takes time. A company called Alpha Coatings, based in Fostoria, Ohio, was already doing a thriving business in auto seals, with a successful line of low-friction coatings it called Resilon.

Alpha had started out in the business of applying adhesive coatings for rubber-to-metal bonding processes used on military vehicles, but in order to grow its business, the company needed to move beyond purely military applications.

"Alpha was formerly privately owned by a gentleman named Terry White," explained Tim Schuette, Whitford's North America operations manager. "He was an entrepreneur, a very smart guy."

White had been purchasing coatings from other companies and applying them, but they weren't providing what he needed.

"White was frustrated," Schuette said. "He felt the suppliers just weren't doing enough R&D. He had some acquaintances who were chemists, started following their advice, mixing some things together and making coatings of his own. He developed the Resilon line himself."

In the mid-2000s, Whitford had developed some coatings for automotive seals, but the coatings hadn't been all that successful.

"They were not very good," Dave Willis said, "and they were nearly all solvent-borne, which was not the first choice of the auto industry. Alpha made better coatings that were waterborne, using mostly different raw materials."

Alpha's potential was impressive enough for Whitford to buy the company in 2006.

"We bought it with the idea that it was a pilot lab," Willis said. "It turned out to be much more than that, and the sales grew quickly in Europe, especially in Germany with the higher-end companies. That most of the coatings were waterborne was a major selling point. We were also able to negotiate better prices with the major suppliers."

Working with the Resilon chemistry also fit within Whitford's long-running operating model, with Whitford's R&D expanding the line by making Resilon coatings for specific customer needs.

Alpha as in Applicator

There was an added benefit to the Alpha acquisition. Alpha is unique among Whitford companies because it not only manufactures coatings but is an applicator as well.

"Alpha does custom work," Tim Schuette said. "If a customer has a seal going on a car that needs one of our coatings, and the customer is not equipped to coat it, nor willing to spend the money for the equipment, the company will send the part to us. We do this for tier one manufacturers that provide the seals for original equipment manufacturers. Since a lot of seal manufacturers try to do as much as they can in house, that makes it challenging for us. If we are going to get this work, we have to be sure of our products, and we have to be fast and efficient in delivering them. We use a lot of state-of-the art automation to get this done."

Whether the Resilon coatings are applied by Alpha or by Alpha's customers, the coatings end up in the vehicles of automotive companies in the United States and overseas, including some of the signature vehicles of General Motors, Ford, and Chrysler.

"For example, we do seals for the Mustang, Ford's flagship vehicle," Schuette said. "Furthermore, one of our biggest accomplishments recently was our coatings being selected for use on all the new Ford F-150 trucks, the best-selling vehicle built in the United States."

While getting Resilon coatings on the F-150 was a huge win, it also created a lot of pressure for Alpha, because Ford had committed a lot to what was a potentially risky, brand-new design, based on a lighter-weight aluminum body.

"The last thing we needed was for Ford to say, 'We have a problem,'" Schuette said. "We were called a couple of times when they were testing trucks and said they'd heard a noise. So we'd go and listen. At times it was a design problem, some geometric issues with the truck, or the coating wasn't applied properly. Original equipment manufacturers, Ford especially, lean heavily on their suppliers to help solve problems."

The automotive world is one of constant challenges within a business universe that never stops evolving, often in the most dramatic ways. Witness the moves toward hybrid and all-electric vehicles.

"With those alternative-energy vehicles, quiet becomes even more of a premium," Schuette said. "The seals have to be extremely quiet because the cars are so quiet themselves."

Ratcheting Up the Flexible Finishes Business

The Alpha Coatings business significantly ratcheted up the flexible finishes part of Whitford's business.

"It was very instrumental in bringing a portfolio of products to the market," said Michael Coates, Whitford's worldwide business development manager. "Our growth in flexible finishes has been quite significant. For example, one product portfolio associated with Alpha grew from nothing in 2006 to $20 million in 2015."

Oven at Alpha Coatings curing rubber automotive components after coating has been applied.

Alpha's products are on vehicles coming out of the factories of automobile manufacturers all over the world, from North and South America to Europe and Asia. Among them are General Motors, Ford, Volkswagen, Daimler (including Mercedes-Benz), BMW, Fiat Chrysler, Renault-Nissan, Toyota, Honda, Hyundai Motor, and Suzuki, to name just a few.

Numerous tier one extruder customers apply Whitford coatings to components headed for those automotive manufacturers, including some of the largest throughout the world. Among those are Cooper Standard Automotive, Henniges Automotive, Hutchinson, SaarGummi Group, Toyoda Gosei, Hwaseung R&A Automotive Parts Co, Magna International, Kinugawa Rubber Industrial, Standard Profil, and Sealynx Automotive, once again to name just a few.

All these companies use Alpha coatings to improve the performance properties of their rubber and plastic parts, adding value to those components. These include reduced friction, noise suppression, freeze/ice release, abrasion resistance, chemical resistance, long-term durability, weather resistance, and a consistent, aesthetically pleasing appearance.

Given that Alpha already has a major presence in the automotive market, how does the company find new uses for its products and continue to grow the business?

"As vehicles further develop and all their features are enhanced, our coatings find their way onto new automotive parts that weren't previously coated," explained Michael Pinter, the company's North American business manager. "One example of this is vehicle interiors becoming quieter and quieter, with our coatings now used on the seals that run along the window line inside and out, where the glass passes into the door. These seals generally are used to wipe the glass as you open and close the window in the Ford Mustang, F-150, Expedition, Fiesta, and Lincoln Navigator. And this is from just this one major manufacturer. The number of these vehicle programs will continue to grow as more and more automobile manufacturers discover the value added to their vehicles with our coatings for these parts."

Selling Alpha products involves a multipronged approach (i.e., selling to both the auto companies and the extruders) at several levels within their organizations. This approach includes interaction with technicians, chemists, engineers, program teams, purchasing departments, lab personnel, and so forth. The effectiveness of the sales team members also involves an intimate understanding of the industry in terms its practitioners can relate to on all levels.

"We do program/platform-based selling," Pinter explained. "That is, we have specific targets, in most cases high-volume-selling vehicles. Also, if you know the automotive industry, you know that we often speak our own language. Whitford/Alpha Coatings team members are well versed in this automotive language and culture, and we speak to our customers in those terms, using their common abbreviations, code names for parts and vehicles, and so on. Most members of our team also have many years of experience in the automotive industry, including having worked at tier one extruders. We know the business processes, from the time a coating gets applied to a part all the way to when the part gets installed on the vehicle. In fact, we are often invited by tier one extruder companies and the automobile manufacturers themselves to come into their assembly plants to see our coatings applied to the parts, then the parts installed on the vehicles."

A Truly Global Coatings Market

For the past several years, automotive has been Whitford's fastest-growing market, and the company's approach to that business is practiced around the world. Close attention to customer needs via high visibility again serves Whitford well.

"Our coatings for rubber car-door seals are used by almost every global carmaker from Ford to Bugatti," said Stephen Butler, Whitford's global business manager for the automotive market, based in the United Kingdom. "We spend a great deal of time at the car companies working to get our coatings specified, as well as at the rubber extruders who purchase our coatings. We are extremely close to the market. Sometimes we are asked to help write specifications, and some of the extruders ask us to make joint visits with them to the car companies."

Given today's truly global business operations, relationships in one part of the world can generate business opportunities continents away.

"Our biggest customers are tier one global extruders," explained Andrew Melville, Whitford's director of South American operations, based in São Paulo, Brazil. "It is a combination of local direct selling and specification selling where applications with international customers in other parts of the world are leveraged here."

The Metal Coatings Business

While the quiet ride, facilitated by the flexible finishes, greatly enhances the driving experience, the quiet would be irrelevant without the ride itself, facilitated by dry lubricants for metal components.

Today, Xylan coatings are used in millions of cars exiting auto factories around the world. There seems to be no limit to the variety of functions these coatings can perform in motor vehicles. Different Xylan coatings solve different problems by providing dry-film lubrication, uniform coefficient of friction, stick/slip prevention, resistance to corrosion and chemicals, reliable freeze release, and so on. Xylan coatings are specified for crash tubes, mounting brackets/plates, cam plates, capsules, shafts, column-locking mechanisms, and on and on.

Being part of the year-to-year design changes of new autos is a lucrative business. However, if you pay attention to the auto industry as closely as Whitford does, sometimes you find external forces provide new marketing opportunities. For example, a major factor in the redesign of the Ford F-150 was to meet the new federal corporate average fuel economy (CAFE) standards—the first bold step by a major manufacturer, which was destined to force changes at all other automotive manufacturers as well.

"The CAFE standards present a lot of options for us," explained Charlie Fields, a Whitford sales manager. "Our products reduce friction, a major factor in fuel economy. Wherever you reduce friction, you are saving fuel. Anywhere we can reduce parasitic loss due to friction, we have a play. That includes components necessary to keep an engine running—transmissions, drive shafts, oil pumps—but consume power from the engine. We've proven significant fuel economy savings by employing coatings on these components."

Also, the Ford-F150's emphasis on lighter-weight components created an additional opportunity for Whitford.

"When you go to alloys, steel fasteners and rivets are used," Fields said. "There need to be coatings to help insulate a steel alloy from an aluminum part to prevent galvanic corrosion."

Regulations will present ongoing challenges, according to Fields. "A raw material may be changed due to a regulation, and that can cause turmoil," he said, "but we are agile enough that we can hit the market sooner with a better product when these opportunities arise, by making sure we are on top of those situations in the marketplace. Our quick response is what leads to our success. Via our agility, we are the first to give the customers what they need."

That agility also applies across Whitford's global network.

"We see opportunity in metal and plastic components to replace other methods of wet and dry lubrication," Whitford Brazil's Andrew Melville explained. "Also, increasing the durability of lighter-weight components will likely become more important."

Starting Slowly, Then Picking Up the Pace

Whitford's movement into the automotive market, however, was more of a slow and steady pace than a dramatic leap. The company rode the wave, in a small way, as lubrication moved from oils and greases to dry-film coatings over the last quarter century. But in selling to small coaters, the company was late in catching the boat of the big changes going on at the time, concentrating efforts instead on the consumer goods market, where it was having more success and experiencing greater growth.

"When you are a smaller company, you have to be very strategic as to where you put your time and effort," Charlie Fields explained. "Most of our automotive applications occurred in the '70s, when Whitford was focused on other industrial markets, because that's where the pull was coming from. Back in the '80s, Whitford focused on getting into the consumer business, because that's where the volume was. Things started to change when we became a larger company. Knowing we could diversify gave us more clout."

Instead of just working directly with the coaters that provided the solutions to customer needs, as Whitford had done historically for the automotive industry, the company began calling on the end users as well, developing specifications at the Fords and GMs and all the tiers involved in making specifications for the coatings. Calling on the people who were writing the specs was a translation of the success Whitford had had in the oil and gas industry.

"We develop relationships with the brand owners," Fields explained. "They create the demand, then the coaters throughout the world apply Whitford coatings. Basically, we listen to the customer who has a problem and we provide the solution, even though the guy who owns the brand and is making the final sale never writes out the check to Whitford. We get in front of these customers, whether through marketing activity or personal contact; then we are able to respond with proper product offerings. Sometimes that also includes being able to help along the entire supply chain through to the end users."

A Change in Mentality
The ever-increasing greenhouse-gas-reduction requirements facing the auto industry that Whitford can help solve—friction, abrasion, wear, corrosion, and the like—are where specialist

fluoropolymer coatings have a lot to offer. Furthermore, auto companies confronted with these kinds of challenges are global and prefer to work with companies like Whitford that have both automotive credibility and global production capabilities. Such a worldwide presence is absolutely critical to gaining, maintaining, and expanding business relationships in the auto industry.

Pistons benefit from Xylan coatings.

"The big change in our mentality in the last couple of years has been getting back to what we are really good at, which is working closely with customers to solve their technical problems," explained Martin Garnett, managing director of Whitford UK's manufacturing facility in Runcorn. "This means concentrating on areas with real friction and abrasion issues, not just steering columns, locks and latches, which just need dry-film coatings. It means coatings for pistons, rods, plates, and bearing surfaces inside the heating and air-conditioning systems, as well as surfaces in the engine units. To do this at the highest level, we purchased a $170,000 Bruker testing machine, and results from this have been instrumental in showing our potential customers how superior our products are to what they have been using."

Once again, changes in regulations worked to Whitford's benefit.

In 2003, the European Union implemented restriction of hazardous substances (RoHS) standards, mandating collection schemes for heavy metals such as lead, mercury, cadmium, and hexavalent chromium. Such metals had been used in coatings in the automotive industry, particularly cadmium in fasteners. However, with Xylan, the OEMs and the coaters have an organic material to replace the heavy metal.

"RoHS dictates when a car gets junked and starts deteriorating into the earth, there is nothing in the coatings that is going to contaminate the ground," said John Russo, Whitford's USA lab manager. "Heavy metal and corrosion-resistant pigments are the easiest ways to get the needed performance characteristics, but since you can't use them because of the regulations, you have to formulate around that. No one has the Holy Grail of automotive fastener coatings, but it becomes a matter of how close you can get to it. Each year it does get better, however, as the raw-material suppliers come out with better corrosion-resistant pigments that do not contain heavy metals. That helps get us closer to the ultimate goal."

In any examination of Whitford's corporate history, the word "opportunity" comes up again and again. Where the opportunities arise and what they look like have been as varied as the complexities spread across the global business landscape. How they are identified and dealt with is what has made Whitford such a success.

While concentrating on the energy aspects of its industrial business when the growth opportunities were there—and on the cookware/bakeware/small-appliance aspects when the opportunities were there—business in the automotive sector was starting to present opportunities heretofore too small to get a lot of attention at the company. But eventually, opportunities in automotive were gaining highway speed.

Where there are challenges in a business sector and you have or can create the products to address those challenges, you have a potential match. Actually creating a match is a matter of staying on top of your game. There are about ten thousand moving components in the average auto being built today. Whitford's Resilon and Xylan coatings are currently used on more than one hundred platforms. Given the ever-increasing number of enhancements that become part of auto designs each year, "opportunity" would appear to be destined to remain the operative word for Whitford's connection to the auto industry for years to come.

CHAPTER 9

Energy's Shifting Winds

> *Parties recognize the importance of averting, minimizing and addressing loss and damage associated with the adverse effects of climate change, including extreme weather events and slow onset events, and the role of sustainable development in reducing the risk of loss and damage.*
> —Article 8, Paris Climate Agreement, December 12, 2015

Representatives of 195 nations gathered in Paris in December 2015 in an effort to set the world on a course to diminish the greenhouse gases they view as having growing effects on a warming planet headed for a disastrous future. Where there is a lack of consensus on the issue of man's effect on global warming, the parties line up on opposite sides of energy generated by fossil fuels or renewable sources: coal, oil, and gas versus sun, wind, and water. The conclusion of an agreement among such a broad representation of countries was a dramatic statement that the way the planet uses energy needed to change.

"It's very hard to go backward from something like this," Nancy Pfund, managing partner of DBL Partners, a venture capital firm that focuses on environmental and economic development, told *The New York Times*. "People are boarding this train, and it's time to hop on if you want to have a thriving twenty-first century economy."[4]

That conclusion had resonance in the investment community. In an extensive report titled "The Low Carbon Economy," Goldman Sachs stated "Between 2015 and 2020, solar and onshore wind will likely add more to the global energy supply than US shale oil production did from 2010 to 2015. By 2025, the market for hybrid and electric vehicles could multiply tenfold. And by 2020, six in ten light bulbs will be LEDs. So it's safe to say the low carbon economy is growing." The investment firm also reported that the market size of low-carbon technologies was in excess of $600 billion in 2015, roughly the size of the US defense budget.

For most of its existence, Whitford has done very well selling coatings for all manner of components used on machinery in the oil and gas industry. Clearly, the consensus reached at the Paris meetings and the wording of the resultant agreement portend a long-term movement away from fossil fuels. But, if Whitford has shown anything since the birth of the company more than fifty years ago, it has been resilience, an ability to adapt to changes, even the most dramatic ones.

The basis of all types of hardware designed to address the needs of energy industries, whether fossil fuels or renewable, are the nuts and bolts that hold it all together, both figuratively and

---

[4] Clifford Krauss and Keith Bradsher, "A Signal to Industry to Go Green in an Era of Carbon Reduction, *The New York Times*, December 13, 2015.

literally. Also, where there are moving parts, friction increases fuel consumption and the attendant loss of power-generating efficiency. Whether they are static fasteners or moving parts, the needs associated with them are addressed by fluoropolymer coatings, and Whitford is the manufacturer of the largest, most complete line of such coatings. Therefore, the need for those coatings will be as important to the success of machinery for renewable energy as it has been for fossil fuels.

Some Historical Perspective

Whitford's relationship with the Oil Patch goes way back. Servicing the oil and gas industry was among the company's earliest successes. Houston, Texas, is the gravitational center of the oil and gas industry. The major oil-field companies have headquarters there. Houston is also where exploration equipment is designed and specifications are written. Further, the specs tend to have a universality to their applications, so they apply to equipment at sites all over the world. Having your product specified opens up potentially lucrative sales with energy providers like ExxonMobil, Shell, BP, and Chevron, as well as with energy industry equipment suppliers like Cameron, Halliburton, and GE Oil and Gas, all of which have thousands of employees at multiple locations around the world.

If, in the earliest days after its development, Xylan 1010 was a solution in search of a problem, Whitford could not have intentionally set out to create a product that seemed so perfectly designed to address the needs of the oil and gas industry. Prior to Whitford's arrival on the scene, the traditional protection for the nuts and bolts on an oil rig was a combination of phosphate and oil. While this combination worked for a while, eventually it would corrode, the seal would be breached, rust would develop, and the nut would loosen. Addressing this issue was critical for the industry.

"There was a $200 million piece of equipment on a deep-water drilling rig that failed," explained Craig Smith, who was part of the Whitford oil and gas industry sales team early on. "The top bolt failed and then the next one and so on until it just unzipped and fell off the rig into the sea. You do not want to be the person who specified that bolt."

The qualities of resistance to wear and low friction are critical for the bolts and nuts used in flanges, pipelines, pumps, and valves for offshore and downhole equipment. Coating both the nut and the threads of the screw with a Xylan fluoropolymer provides a much more secure and longer-lasting seal.

A Market for Whitford's Unique Selling Approach

From the outset, members of the Whitford sales team were convinced they had the product for numerous oil and gas equipment applications, but success would come only if they could convince customers to try it, buy it, and use it. Winning oil and gas business then became a principal target for Whitford's unique approach to specification selling.

Team members didn't position this as a sales effort, but as an opportunity to educate prospective buyers. Convince customers that when they specified a Whitford product, they would have good reasons why it would work and do what it was supposed to do. Team members conducted "lunch and learn" sessions with individual companies. These sessions were typically held in a company conference room with as many as fifty attendees. Theirs was a soft-sell approach.

Sales team members avoided PowerPoint presentations that would come off as slick and hard selling; instead, they used a white board, making the presentation more natural, less rehearsed, and pointedly responsive to the specific audience. They understood that oil and gas engineers, while keenly interested in innovation, nonetheless needed to be convinced a product was absolutely reliable.

"The engineering mentality is not impressed with a flashy sales pitch or high pressure," explained Brian Willis, who had spent a great deal of his career in Houston, then moved on to head Whitford's inside-sales efforts. "Rather, the most successful approach is to be helpful, to provide solutions to problems, and to always be reasonable and logical."

This can take time and requires patience, but it is the approach Whitford has always taken toward selling, beginning with those very early days. While Whitford's message was a strong one, persistence in delivering that message was also critical to making a sale. For example, team members had been in touch with an engineer at a major oil company for years, and although they had called on him regularly, there had been no significant sales. The prospect engineer eventually moved to another company where he had greater authority in that incarnation. This time, he bought and ended up becoming an important repeat customer for Whitford. Pressuring him when he was not really in a position to buy could well have alienated him.

To solidify Whitford's relationship with oil and gas industry suppliers, the company didn't limit its approach to simply calling on the fastener producers. The sales team made joint calls with those suppliers and their end users. In a relatively short period,

Whitford products were specified by many Gulf Coast oil and chemical facilities. Today, the company continues to sell Xylan 1010 and its derivatives to this market each year, at ever-increasing volumes.

Tilting at Windmills?

"The world of energy is seeing major change," BP's Chairman Carl-Henric Svanberg said, addressing an industry conference in late 2015. "Change brings challenges and opportunities. Some are economic, some are technological, and others are environmental. But they are connected, often with long-term consequences. The energy industry has an obvious, but not simple, long-term task and challenge. And that is to supply the world with the energy it needs to drive development and economic growth while doing so sustainably."

Dave Willis began paying attention to sustainable energy and its business potential for Whitford in the industry's equipment needs well before the movement had built the head of steam it had going into the Paris climate negotiations. After all, there are thousands of nuts and bolts in modern windmill designs, and they all need to be coated. Furthermore, the fasteners being used in some of the earlier designs had an inherent flaw. They were coated with zinc flake for corrosion resistance and wax for lubricant to aid in fastening or tightening the nuts. When the fasteners remained in storage for an extended period of time, gravity caused the wax lubricant to flow slowly around the fastener, ending up with more on the underside. Consequently, when the fastener was tightened, the friction between the nut and bolt was uneven. That inequality caused the fastener to loosen, sometimes in just months, so it had to be retightened periodically, at significant cost and multiple man-hours. The inefficient solution to this problem was to use fasteners that were much larger than needed and much more difficult to fasten uniformly.

"The oil industry tackled this problem nearly fifty years ago," Willis explained. "They use our lubricated coating Xylan, which provides both corrosion resistance and uniform lubrication in one application. Furthermore, Xylan is capable of functioning across a broad range of temperatures, from subzero liquid-nitrogen to hundreds of degrees Fahrenheit. The binder resin has good corrosion resistance, but the most important part is the coated area under the nuts. It does not corrode, so it can be loosened with a wrench, rather than a blowtorch. Today, a Xylan-coated bolt is not only the preferred way to fasten an object on an oil platform, it is effectively the only way."

Xylan coatings battle corrosion; removal is easy with a wrench instead of a blowtorch.

Unfortunately, the wind-power industry had been stuck in its ways for a considerable time, not even entertaining the possibility of a new, much more efficient solution. Willis felt the decision-makers in the industry would eventually come around because the Xylan coating solution would save them millions of dollars and make their jobs much easier. The challenge was how to get them to that point.

Consequently, Whitford commissioned a ten-year study to assess the "long-term atmospheric exposure of corrosion protection systems with Xylan as a topcoat." It was conducted by DNV-GL, a highly respected international certification and classification organization based in Norway.

Completed in late 2015, the study's conclusions as to the effect of Xylan fluoropolymer topcoat on breakout torque was "lower and with less scatter compared to the same coatings without topcoat." It further concluded that "most coating systems with high potential for long-term service life comprised a fluoropolymer topcoat (i.e., different Xylan variations)."

"The report makes its point in our favor," Willis explained. On the other hand, Willis disagreed with one of the evaluators' conclusions that fasteners continue to use zinc with the coatings "unless it is a very special situation. We think you can get the same or better results cheaper and faster and with less potential metallic corrosion with Xylan. And the maintenance of a Xylan system is a fraction of the cost of the current system being used. Our coatings do not need the annual retightening of the nuts that the combination of the zinc and its nonuniformity demand."

Persistent Pursuit of Opportunity

There will always be pockets of resistance to changes in established procedures. Nonetheless, given the attention the global climate meeting generated, with its focus on the shift to renewable energy sources expected to increase, perhaps exponentially, persistence once again remains an integral element in Whitford's longer-term strategy. It is also extremely important to understand the geographic arenas in which the company is actively involved.

"Understanding the European geopolitical environment, where renewable energies are concerned, is important," explained Gareth Berry, who is responsible for the specification of Whitford products in the UK continental shelf and North Sea oil and gas sector. "The EU has enshrined in legislation CO_2 emission reduction figures, submitted by national governments, all the way through to 2030, and there are arbitrary penalties if these aren't met."

Again, the shifting sands of politics put pressure on the EU to seek forms of greater energy independence.

"There is a significant reduction in nuclear power generation in Europe, combined with a reduction of coal power stations in favor of existing or newly commissioned natural gas stations," Berry said. "Much of Europe is dependent on Russian gas supply, one pipeline of which is routed through Ukraine, which has been involved in a political standoff and tense military posturing with Russia. The UK is stuck at the end of this line. Not great for energy security. The savior of sorts is the North Sea with coastlines in the UK, France, Holland, Belgium, Denmark, and Norway."

Two factors make the North Sea particularly suited for offshore wind generation. The sea is fairly shallow, with maximum seabed depths in the southern and northern areas at fifty meters and two hundred meters, respectively. The more shallow the sea, the fewer challenges in foundation installation. Second, the prevailing winds are strong, especially in winter when the demand for power is greatest. Consequently, more than twenty-five hundred wind turbines have been installed in the North Sea, with more than seven thousand expected by 2020.

Onshore and offshore wind generated a record 11 percent of the United Kingdom's electricity in 2015, up from 9.5 percent the year before, according to RenewableUK, an organization that describes itself "as a catalyst for policy change to support the deployment of wind, wave and tidal energy and seeks to maximize their benefits to the UK as a whole." In early 2016, its policy director, Dr. Gordon Edge, told the *Daily Mail*, "This is a great way to start the new year. The wind industry can be proud that it has shattered weekly, monthly, quarterly and annual generation records in 2015."[5]

So where do Whitford products fit into the scheme of things? Whitford coatings are used in the manufacture of turbine blades by the major suppliers.

"Every turbine has three blades, which can range in length from forty-nine meters to eighty-five meters," Berry explained. "The blades are a composite, consisting mainly of glass fiber, balsa wood, and resin. Molds are used to produce these blades. Whitford's coated glass cloth is used to line the molds of the largest offshore wind turbine manufacturer. The coating aids with release of each blade once all the resins are cured."

Further, Whitford Xylan coatings on threaded fasteners throughout the turbine structure inhibit corrosion and deliver a dry lubricant with a very low, long-lasting coefficient of friction.

"This provides excellent torque-to-load ratios," Berry said, "which is particularly important when you have three eighteen-ton blades whirling around at high speed, with the only thing

---

[5] Press Association, "Wind Power Shatters Energy Generation Records," *Daily Mail*, January 5, 2016.

connecting them to the turbine hub a number of fasteners in a flange joint."

While offshore wind farms have the advantage of more frequent and powerful winds and less negative visual impact on the landscape, their construction costs are considerably higher. Furthermore, offshore sites pose problems in terms of accessibility for routine maintenance issues. Xylan coatings, used throughout the structure, help drive down the "life-operating" costs by reducing maintenance over the twenty-five-year life span typically demanded.

Moving with the Tides

The earth's gravitational relationship with the moon causes tidal streams. This tidal movement creates the potential for a form of energy that can be converted into electrical power. Furthermore, any constriction of these streams can produce high-velocity tidal flows that are even more effective for energy generation. Given the enormous potential of this source of power, the European Union has supported ocean energy research and development for many years. Since 1988, the EU has funded more than forty projects on renewable energy, including offshore wind, tidal, and wave power.

One of the world's most wild and isolated places is the Orkney Islands, part of an archipelago ten miles from the coast of northern Scotland. Although well off the beaten track, the islands are home to cutting-edge wave and tidal technology that is not only helping change the mix of the world's energy sources but also creating jobs and helping remote communities prosper.

The European Marine Energy Centre has been leading the development of technology to harness this energy. Established in 2003, EMEC is the first and only center of its kind to provide developers of both wave and tidal energy converters with purpose-built, accredited, open-sea testing facilities. Although this form of energy generation has not received the attention that solar and wind power have, tides are more predictable than either and not weather-related.

Tidal turbines with Xylan work like underwater windmills.

"EMEC is a leading global test site in both tidal and wave energy generation, giving developers the facilities to test devices from components up to full scale, with grid connection for power takeoff," Berry explained. "We were first introduced to EMEC in 2011 and have developed a progressively closer relationship over the ensuing years. So much so that they are very much advocates for Whitford, having introduced us to several of the leading tidal developers."

Tidal turbines work like underwater windmills, with the ebb and flow of the tides forcing the blades to spin, thereby generating electricity. In August of 2011, Atlantis Resources successfully connected its one-megawatt tidal turbine to the United Kingdom's power grid, with Xylan an integral part of the system. The new tidal turbine uses Xylan 1424 on the heavy bolts and washers that secure the hatch covers. Xylan was chosen over a multicoat marine system, since Xylan permits the easy removal and refitting of the coated metal parts and provides excellent resistance to the harsh elements to which the parts are constantly exposed.

The Atlantis turbine operates at a depth of about fifty meters (about half the length of a football field). The tides are strong in the North Atlantic—about four meters per second (equivalent to 7.8 knots, or nine miles per hour). But there is also the severe, corrosive saltwater atmosphere, so Whitford's Xylan has been specified to resist the extreme environment.

To date, the results of using Xylan have been so promising that EMEC has permitted Whitford to create its own underwater test site for further experimentation in energy generation by tidal forces.

Catching the Wave

Wave-power technology is also gaining an increasing level of interest. When wind causes water to move near the sea surface, the height of the wave peaks and the time between successive peaks can be used to generate energy. Offshore wave converters are designed for deep sites, while shoreline and near-shore systems are modified for shallower water. The power-generating devices are usually floating, and the splash zone is where the most demanding corrosive conditions are experienced.

"Tidal technology is in a far more advanced state than wave, but in both sectors, our coatings are used in the areas of corrosion inhibition and dry lubrication, particularly on threaded components and valves," Berry said. "After eighteen months planning, we launched our own coating test site for this technology at EMEC in October 2014."

During the first stage of the project, Whitford is testing coated panels and bolts at the EMEC location at Stromness Harbour in the Orkney Islands. The brightly colored test panels can be seen on the side of the pier at low tide. The panels and bolts are part of a coatings test program taking place to analyze existing and developmental coating products under harsh environments—in this case, the splash zone.

"The pier provides a good representation of a splash zone," Berry explained. "Part of a structure that is intermittently exposed to air and immersed in the sea, subject to a range of wet and dry conditions, as the test pieces are submerged and covered in line with the tidal ebb and flow. The pier provides an accessible location that can be easily reached and regularly monitored. Panels and bolts not only provide suitable test pieces when fixing them to the pier structure, but they also offer a standardized method in which to assess the performance of the coating. As the surface and coating conditions remain the same, the only changeable factor is the time that the test pieces are exposed."

Whitford's aim is to record high-quality live test data. The real environment perfectly depicts the conditions in which the coatings will be used. Data received will be key in the promotion of Whitford coatings to multiple sectors including marine energy and offshore wind, as well as oil and gas. The company's relationship with EMEC is open ended, with Whitford expecting to keep the test panels and bolts in place for up to seven years.

Battling Corrosive Effects

Resistance to corrosion is a major issue for all renewable energy equipment, especially given that most spend their operating existence exposed to the elements, in many cases under the harshest conditions. The turbines that power tidal or wave technology equipment run at or below the surface of the sea. More and more wind-powered equipment is being located miles off seacoasts, attached to the seabed, deep below the surface in highly corrosive salt water. Even wind farms located on land are exposed to the elements. Ditto for solar-powered equipment. All of the aforementioned factors play well for Whitford coatings, which have proven their long-term benefits in the harshest of climates.

Corrosion comes in many forms, among them atmospheric, galvanic, chemical, fretting, and salt fog. Stainless-steel fasteners often have been specified for heavy equipment, but when applied to equipment in coastal environments, they are susceptible to chlorine-induced stress cracking, a form of chemical corrosion. Xylan-coated carbon-steel bolts, on the other hand, are not similarly affected.

The upside of stainless-steel fasteners—they generate an oxide surface film that provides corrosion protection—can prove to be a negative in hostile environments. When a stainless-steel fastener is tightened, and pressure builds between the contacting and sliding thread surfaces, the protective oxide can be broken. This galling often results in the metal surfaces locking together and seizing. If the tightening continues, the fastener can be twisted off.

Stainless-steel fasteners need to be retorqued after twenty-four hours due to galling, losing up to 40 percent of their clamping force. Xylan-coated carbon-steel fasteners reach the required clamp load on the first makeup. The corrosion-protection properties of Xylan coating systems greatly reduce breakout torque, enabling users to remove the fasteners without causing damage to parts. Furthermore, from an economic perspective, stainless-steel fasteners can cost twice as much as Xylan-coated carbon-steel fasteners.

When dissimilar metals come into contact, galvanic corrosion can result. Xylan-coated carbon steel in combination with any alloy does not lead to galvanic corrosion. Xylan coatings, particularly the formulations made with PTFE, offer a simple solution to the problem. Xylan insulates one metal from the other, shielding them from compounds such as salts, acids, or bases.

Crevice corrosion occurs in confined spaces, such as gaps and contact areas between parts, under gaskets or seals, inside cracks and seams, and so on. Xylan's ability to withstand the harsh environmental conditions in offshore wind, wave, and tidal applications makes it a perfect partner for the marine renewables sector.

"We are also involved in solar cell manufacturing with molds and applications for fasteners, working with a company making flexible circuit boards for solar panels," Brian Willis said.

Strong Standing in Both Markets

Although the events of 2015 generated a great deal of attention to perceived problems in the world's dependence on fossil fuels and a need to shift to renewable forms of energy, even those who are most vocal about the transformation understand it will be a gradual process. Dealing with the dynamics of that shift drives the strategy at Whitford, both long term and near term.

"Although not yet a great percentage of our business, Whitford has been selling into alternative energy applications, and that potential is growing," explained Bill Pernice, the company's global business manager, energy and construction. "We continue to position Whitford products where applicable and where it makes sense to expend resources. We have been and are continuing to test and qualify our products into these applications, all in an effort to prepare for the future."

That the major Oil Patch companies were already straddling the fence between the two approaches to energy generation was apparent during and immediately after the Paris negotiations. Full-page ads and TV spots emphasizing that position were ubiquitous.

"If you look at one of our biggest users, ExxonMobil, its advertising explained exactly what they are doing," Brian Willis said. "The engineers I am particularly familiar with are looking into all these markets, not just oil and gas, and they are using our coatings for everything they are doing. So these contacts are automatically giving us a foot in the door into these new markets."

If keeping an eye on future markets, having the resilience to create products for emerging markets, and maintaining the persistence to go after that business are all key elements in

Whitford's sales strategy, a sense of balance is also necessary in addressing market shifts. While opportunities in the movement to renewable energy are on the horizon, Whitford's oil and gas business remains a major source of revenue for the present.

"In fact, renewable energy opportunities complement our oil and gas business," Pernice said. "While renewable energy sources are growing, fossil fuel will continue to provide a large percentage of our energy production, at least in our lifetime. As the variety of energy sources are expanding, we will be able to benefit from having a strong standing in both markets."

CHAPTER 10

BUILDING THE BUSINESS OF COOKWARE AND BAKEWARE

You will never get out of a pot or pan anything fundamentally better than what went into it.
—MARTHA MCCULLOCH-WILLIAMS, DISHES
& BEVERAGES OF THE OLD SOUTH

Each February, forty eight hundred exhibitors from more than ninety countries set up their display booths at Ambiente, a huge housewares trade show in Frankfurt, Germany. They present the latest design trends and innovations in an industry that accounts for more than $330 billion in sales worldwide, more than $75 billion of that in the United States alone. Exhibitors feature a wide range of design concepts and showcase all manner of products and furnishing accessories for the table, the kitchen, and the rest of the household, as well as decorative products, gift articles, jewelry, and wellness and fashion accessories.

The show attracts more than one hundred thirty thousand trade visitors from more than one hundred fifty countries. Buyers and sellers at all levels in the supply chain navigate the exhibits; interact in meeting rooms, dining areas, nooks and crannies throughout the huge convention center; and retreat to off-site hotel hospitality suites for cocktails and conversation. They make new contacts, exchange ideas, discover new material sources and potential markets for their products and services, renew established business relationships, and cut deals.

Exhibiting at the International Home and Housewares Show in Chicago.

One month later, in early March, the venue shifts to Chicago for the International Home and Housewares Show, another key home-goods business marketplace. The numbers for this show are roughly half those of Ambiente; nonetheless, the twenty one hundred exhibitors from more than forty countries attract more than sixty thousand total attendees from one hundred twenty five countries.

Whitford exhibits in both places, the presence at each an endorsement of how the home-goods market has grown in importance for the company. Along with the obvious sales and marketing opportunities such gatherings present to companies that sell their wares to the housewares industry, such shows also provide logistical benefits to a company like Whitford by bringing together teams of its own employees, who otherwise are spread out all over the world.

"Trade shows give us an opportunity to get the issues in front of us, all together in one place," said Jim Gibian, Whitford's worldwide consumer marketing manager. "What's more and more apparent as this industry progresses is that globalization makes the world smaller. In many cases, what we're finding as we become larger is that our customers are much more global in scale. So we have an opportunity to put the European team, the Chinese team, and the US team all together in a room with a customer. The largest brand owners in the world enjoy working with us because wherever they need to produce goods, we have a factory to supply the coatings. You want to produce in India; we're there. You want to produce in Brazil or Colombia; we're there. You want to produce in Europe or in China or Vietnam; we're there. The fact that we can react quickly, wherever they are producing, is an extreme benefit."

The Importance of a Global Identity
Establishing operations at or near key points of contact with its customers was the only option for Whitford's long-term financial health. Therefore, over the years, Whitford has placed a great deal of emphasis on being strategically located within striking distance of where its customers are located.

"So a trade show is just another touchpoint for us to get in front of customers that can benefit from our global scale," Gibian said. "It is a very efficient use of the company's time, energy, resources, and money."

However, renting exhibit space, creating state-of-the-art displays, and flying in personnel from all over the world to attend such shows is expensive. How does a company judge the return on that investment?

"It isn't always a linear relationship," Gibian said. "I look at trade shows as not a return on investment but a return on our ability to see existing customers and meet new ones. They also allow us to discuss with our teams what's happening in the marketplace and to look at trends. It's not so much a matter of return on investment but return on objective. What are our objectives at the trade show, and did we accomplish them? Did we meet with new customers? Did we discuss ongoing projects with existing customers and solve any issues that they might be having?"

Whitford also uses its presence at these shows to provide common meeting space for brand owners and retail customers, applicators, and representatives from the factories that provide product for end users.

"In our meeting rooms, there is an open door for our customers," Gibian explained. "We tell them, 'Come, use our meeting room, and sit down with the factory rep that is making your cookware in China.' The factories appreciate that; customers appreciate that. It's a casual way for them to conduct their business. Also, we can't always get to China or to India to meet with these factories, so it gives us a common spot to meet with them as well."

The Company's Move into the Consumer Side

While Whitford's earliest products were a hit with industrial sectors like oil and gas, the company was gun shy about competing on the consumer side with the Goliath from Delaware. Two facts stood out. The consumer cookware market was clearly owned by the DuPont Teflon name, so much so that "Teflon" had become the generic term for nonstick cookware coatings. And the Teflon brand enjoyed the backing of the giant corporation's marketing muscle. It was also the opinion of Whitford's technical people at the time that the company's Xylan coating, as it was formulated, was not a cookware coating and would not stand up to the rigors of stovetop conditions.

Nonetheless, as Whitford began expanding around the world, it became clear that limiting its product range to industrial coatings was also limiting its ability to grow. Meanwhile, Whitford's R&D efforts to modify its coatings were bearing results that could work for cookware.

When Whitford first decided to approach the cookware market in the early to mid-1970s, an obvious player was Meyer Manufacturing of Hong Kong. Stanley Cheng started the cookware business for Meyer in 1971, when he was in his early twenties, after graduating from Oregon State University in mechanical engineering. While Meyer would seem a name better suited to a German manufacturer, the word "Meyer" phonetically is similar to the Chinese characteristics for America and Asia, which was the focus of Meyer at the time.

From a sales perspective, the prospect of working with Meyer was a matter of it presenting an obvious opportunity, so Dave Willis and a colleague set off to visit with Cheng.

"We began to supply Meyer with our newly developed one-coat Xylan 8300 product. By 1978, Meyer was our largest customer," Willis said. "Then Phillips Petroleum altered the melt flow of its Ryton product from greater than five thousand to less than fifty on the same scale. (See chapter five.) That change translated into taking a smooth coating to a rough one. Since we could not change that, Meyer necessarily went to another supplier in the form of DuPont. It took twenty-three years to become a supplier to Meyer once again."

It is perhaps an ironic twist of fate in Whitford's half-century history that the company's outsize dependence on its Meyer Manufacturing business—about 40 percent by the late '70s—almost led to its undoing. Meyer pulled its business as a result of a change in the characteristics of a coating Whitford supplied, but the problem was a result of an alteration in the Phillips Petroleum resin Whitford used in those coatings. Nonetheless, Whitford's failure to detect the problem and the subsequent loss of the Meyer business pushed the company to the brink of failure. It took Whitford years to win back the business, the result of the company's ever-advancing, ever-improving product line, along with the conviction that persistence in presenting these products to Meyer would ultimately win out. Today, Meyer is once again among Whitford's top customers worldwide.

North to Nordic Ware

On a weekend in January 2016, Dave Willis and US technical director Kurt Mecray left the unusually temperate June-in-January temperatures of Pennsylvania for the subzero cold of Minneapolis. It was not a particularly good weekend for

Minnesotans and their beloved pro football team. With the game-day temperature below zero on the playing field, the hometown Vikings lost a do-or-die playoff game to the visiting Seattle Seahawks on a missed chip-shot field goal with time running out. Willis and Mecray, however, were there for a more uplifting matter. They had come to help celebrate the seventieth anniversary of a company whose business was crucial to Whitford's earliest days.

Northland Aluminum Products was founded in 1946 by Henry Dalquist, newly returned from World War II, and his wife, Dotty. The Dalquists turned an original stake of $500 into what is still a family-owned business that today employs three hundred fifty people at its factory in the Minneapolis suburb of Saint Louis Park. Under its consumer products name, Nordic Ware, it produces a wide range of cookware and bakeware for the oven, toaster oven, stovetop, grill, and microwave. What put the company on the map on a grand scale was the 1950 invention of the Bundt pan, that mountain-shaped metal mold that has baked an endless number of cakes in more than seventy million homes ever since. Ingenious in design, the Bundt pan has fluted sides and a central, chimney-like tube that allows more of the cake mix to touch the surface of the pan, thereby providing faster and more even heat distribution during baking. To keep the baking mix from sticking, the design cried out for a Whitford coating.

"Northland was already a twenty-year-old producer of cookware items in 1969, when we started Whitford Corporation," Willis explained. "The company specialized in bakeware, especially the Bundt pans, the bulk of them sold by mail order from coupons inserted into the flour sales of General Mills."

While DuPont's Teflon was firmly entrenched as the coating for consumer nonstick cookware, Willis felt Whitford could exploit a different opening.

"It was probably 1972 or '73 that I first called on them," he said. "They had a division—still do—that did coatings of industrial products and cookware for other manufacturers. The industrial part was easier to sell, since DuPont was not the same force in industrial products, and Xylan 1010 answered most industrial needs. The relationship developed slowly, as most do."

Eventually, Whitford became the main source of coatings for Northland's industrial products and its go-to coating for the company's cast aluminum Bundt pans. While other coating companies have chipped away at the business, the relationship remained a sound one after more than forty-five years.

"We are two family companies, and we respect each other," Willis said. "What business we have lost is simply good sense on their part. One source is sometimes necessary but seldom good business sense."

Building a Retail Marketing Team

Sometimes the talent finds you. Fran Groesbeck had started her career in product development for Macy's, where she was instrumental in moving the Macy's brand cookware coatings from DuPont's Teflon to Whitford's Quantum2. (See chapter six.) Her contact had been John Badner, then Whitford's director of marketing, and she knew Dave Willis and other Whitford staff members from her attendance at various trade shows.

"By 2000, it was time for a change," she said. "John Badner had become a friend as well as a business associate, and we were catching up on the phone one day when I asked his opinion on my next move. He in turn mentioned that Whitford was interviewing candidates to start a retail program. He said that Whitford employees were great at the technical stuff but couldn't speak 'retailese.'"

Groesbeck was invited to meet with Badner and others to present her ideas on what she would do if she got the position.

"I was so psyched!" she explained. "I loved the Whitford people I worked with over the years and had a secret wish to work for Dave Willis. He is one of a kind, both personally and professionally."

So she went into high gear preparing a PowerPoint presentation for the meeting. She copied Whitford logos from the company website. She put together a whole presentation on how to reach retailers, what they would care about with coatings, and how to get them to specify Whitford.

When she arrived at Whitford's offices, she was led into a meeting room where she confronted five interviewers: Willis and Badner, Tony Weir and Joan Eberhardt of corporate communications, and Mike Miller, Whitford's worldwide technical director.

"I will never forget that split second of fear seeing all those top executives sitting there," she said.

After about an hour, with the presentation and interview completed, she was asked to wait outside the meeting room. A few minutes later, Willis emerged and asked her to come with him to his office.

"I assumed it was for an individual interview," Groesbeck recalled, "but the question he asked wasn't what I expected. What would it take to get me to join Whitford?"

Groesbeck joined Whitford soon after. When you go from demanding customer to new employee, however, there can be some transitional issues.

"While I was at Macy's using Whitford coatings," Groesbeck said, "I made a lot of last-minute and crazy requests for the Whitford labs, especially the one in Singapore. That is what we retailers do. We ask for everything, and we want it yesterday. In our minds, that is totally valid and logical. Color matches, test data, changing from one coating to the next, pricing differences, competitor comparisons—you name it."

After joining Whitford, Groesbeck's very first trip was to see the facility in Singapore. Upon arrival, she was greeted by Kurt Mecray, who was in charge of the lab there. He also had been running the lab during the years Groesbeck was at Macy's, then known by her maiden name, Attilio.

"Unbeknownst to me," she said, "Kurt had worked on many of my projects and had solved many of my problems. We started walking and talking, when he asked me where I had worked previously. I told him that I was the product manager for 'Tools of the Trade' at Macy's."

Before she could finish the last syllable, Mecray turned to her and said, "You're *that* Fran?"

"We had a good laugh about it," she said, "but we talk about that first meeting to this day."

Retail Marketing Program

Getting Whitford to think more in terms of retail and speak that retailese, however, was going to be challenging.

"There was no retail program before I got there," Groesbeck said, "so I had to create it. John Badner in sales, Tony Weir and Joan Eberhardt in corporate communications, helped me at every turn. Mike Miller and Kurt Mecray in the labs were very patient with teaching me what I needed to know about coatings and the technical side of things. I built a database from people I knew in the industry and the retailers we needed to target. We had to build a retail marketing program from scratch."

Having worked on the consumer side, Groesbeck knew the questions product-development managers were likely to ask: Aren't most nonstick coatings the same? How can I achieve lower prices and better margins? Is there a nonstick that will do the job at my price point? Will the coated cookware on my selling floor perform well? Is this nonstick safe for food contact?

With the help of her colleagues in corporate communications and on the technical side of things, a comprehensive retail marketing program was developed with Groesbeck as its head. The program made it far more efficient for Whitford to work actively with retailers and address what they had to contend with on any given day, from the number crunching of the current season to planning the product assortment for two seasons ahead and the pressure of achieving sales projections.

Since the program began in 2000, Whitford's retail marketing team has assisted retailers of coated housewares products in finding the answers to questions about sourcing, regulatory issues, coating performance, overcoming hurdles like meeting deadlines, controlling product quality, and achieving lower prices and better margins, all with the ultimate goal of driving sales.

"I keep my name in front of retailers without being a pest," she said. "Walmart, Target, JC Penney, all the big ones. Even if they don't have a project with us, I keep in contact."

The US retail marketing program has since been replicated in Europe and Asia. The key element to maintaining these relationships has always been building trust.

"We emphasize integrity in what we do," Groesbeck said. "We earn trust because we don't pad or twist. We tell the truth, all the time, even if it's not what customers want to hear. Then we become a reliable source. And they come to us for everything. We become the industry experts they can trust."

The objective of this pull marketing is to convince retailers that when they are talking to their factories about nonstick cookware, they specify Whitford coatings and not leave the selection up to the factory.

"Patience and persistence," Groesbeck said. "It took me five years to get through to the right people at Target, but now Whitford is the coating on all their private-label cookware. Once you make these kinds of connections, it's easier to keep the momentum going. I pull via the retailer; my team in Asia pushes via the factory."

Expanding into Italy

By the late '90s, Dave Willis was looking to expand Whitford's cookware/bakeware business in continental Europe, with a particular interest in Italy. Concurrently, the owners of Becherplast, an Italian manufacturer of such coatings, were seeking ways to expand their business.

Becherplast was founded in 1967 by Attilio Vallaperta in Brescia, an ancient Roman city in northern Italy, not far from Milan. After his death in 1982, Vallaperta's eldest son, Giuseppe (Chicco to family and friends), joined the firm. Five years later, his younger brother, Francesco, joined. During a trade show, Chicco Vallaperta was introduced to Willis, a friendship began, the relationship developed, and in 1998 the companies agreed to merge.

"When we merged the two companies, Becherplast was doing around 1.5 million euros per year," Vallaperta explained. "Since then, thanks to the efforts of all the Whitford people around the world, we have grown dramatically. We run a factory for the European, Middle Eastern and African regions. We have grown because of our strong relationships with our customers and the many new products we have developed together."

Nonetheless, while the merger was crucial to the expansion of Whitford Italy's business, such a decision comes only after a great deal of soul searching, especially, as in the case of Becherplast, where the company has been built from the ground up by a parent particularly proud of his ability to have done so.

"When we decided to sell part of the company, it was tough," Vallaperta said. "We were selling something that had been our father's dream, but in the end, we clearly understood that it was something that had to be done. If you need to grow a company, it's important to find a relationship with another company that can enhance what you do. Whitford not only had the knowledge base but facilities around the world."

The new corporate relationship also got the Vallapertas to think more expansively.

"The merger opened our minds," Chicco Vallaperta said. "Before, we were focused only on the European market. Afterward, we met a lot of new people from different cultures. A Whitford meeting can sometimes feel like the United Nations, and we can all have different points of view. Sometimes we argue. Sometimes we pull in different directions. But in the end, what works for Whitford is good for all of us."

As is the case throughout the company, at Whitford Italy, the emphasis is also on problem-solving.

"That's why you have to be very close to your customers," Vallaperta said. "You need to have the kind of mutual understanding that lets you say to the customer, 'You're doing something wrong' or 'You need to change this or that.' You have to build that level of trust."

Vallaperta emphasized that positive interpersonal relationships apply to employees as well as customers, something he practices from the moment he arrives at his office each morning.

"The first thing I do is to check in on the shop floor," he said. "I walk around the facility at least five or six times a day. I want our people to understand I am there and ready to talk with them. The heart of the company is in production. Each employee must be respected and aware of his or her importance to the company. You could be the most powerful salesman in the world, but if one guy in production doesn't make the product up to standards, you will never be able to sell it. So respect is key."

Marketing in the EU

The European Union, however, presented its own set of marketing challenges.

"The EU brought us the single currency, reduced bureaucracy when conducting business, elimination of tax duties, as well as easy access to neighboring member states," explained Andy Reynolds, Whitford's European retail marketing manager, based at the company's facility in Germany. "However, the consumer culture, mentality, taste, style, language, and retail legal and regulatory requirements in the member states remain different, creating a challenge for the market."

Like Fran Groesbeck in the United States, Reynolds began his career on the consumer side of the coatings market at HP Zenker, one of the largest bakeware manufacturers in Germany, which was using Xylan coatings. In 2003, when Whitford was looking for a consumer sales manager in Germany, he applied for and got the job. A year later he was promoted to retail marketing manager. By that point, it had become clear that the diversity of specific markets within the general unanimity of the European "union" required a marketing program that addressed this demanding situation. Fortunately, the model already existed on the other side of the Atlantic.

"The European marketing program was created in 2004, four years after the successful launch of the retail marketing program in the US," Reynolds said. "This was a logical step, with European retail having many similarities with US retail. The initial countries targeted were Germany, the United Kingdom, and France, all three representing thirty-five percent of the top thirty worldwide retailers. Further established markets were to follow in Spain, Italy, the Scandinavian and East European countries.

With this level of growth, the retail marketing team expanded to include dedicated retail managers in several EU countries."

When meeting with partners, the diverse elements relevant to the specific retail market and retail partner are discussed to help arrive at the best coating for the requirements of each, before the actual cookware or bakeware is produced. Whitford's extensive product range can address consumers' needs, irrespective of their location, taste, style, and income.

"A good-better-best strategy and a large variety of choice in color and design help check all the boxes and fulfill the specific retailer and country requirements," Reynolds said. "Coating innovation, consistency in quality, high technical know-how, customer-orientated flexibility are all paramount. Establishing, cultivating, maintaining, and expanding personal contact with partners and supplying them product information help us to remain at the forefront of the coatings market."

Addressing the Vast Asian Marketplace

Rice is part of the diet of more than two-thirds of the world's population and *the* dominant staple food for the 3.7 billion people who live in Asia. While rice has long been associated with diets in Asia, there is literally no continent where it is not a significant dietary element—its attractiveness ranges from its affordability for the poorest populations to the health consciousness of the more affluent.

While rice cookers had long been considered small kitchen appliances for only one style of food, analyses by *HomeWorld Business* magazine indicate that manufacturers have been repositioning the product as a multifunction unit capable of cooking a variety of foods, which "has helped the category to better align with the growing number of consumers who are looking to eat more healthy day in and day out." The magazine reported huge increases in sales of rice cookers in 2014 and 2015, topping more than $140 million in both years.[6]

Whitford has had a sales office in Hong Kong since 1990, a factory in Singapore since 1993. Over the subsequent two decades, the company expanded to factories in Jiangmen, China, and Bangalore, India; added sales offices in Shanghai and Ningbo in China; and added an office in Hochiminh City, Vietnam. While Whitford's Asia operations are greatly diversified, supplying coatings across a broad spectrum of cookware, bakeware, and small electrics, the company's long-established presence in this part of the world places it at an advantage.

"It may not be as easy for a foreigner to understand or even imagine the potential business in rice cookers in Asia," said Philip Wong. Wong was hired to help set up and run Whitford's Hong Kong office in 1992 and today manages the company's retail activities in all the Asia markets it serves. "When I first joined Whitford, I had to deal with cultural differences that I had not thought of, like the western cooking culture of the nonstick fry pan. So I spent a lot of time explaining why the rice cookware market is as important as the other cookware/bakeware business around the world."

By 1998, Whitford had penetrated the rice-cooker market in China, and Wong saw Whitford's constant innovations in coatings as a principal reason for that and a key element in the company's ongoing competitiveness in this market.

---

[6] "Rice Cookers Retail Unit Sales," *HomeWorld Business*, January 2016

"Our core competence and strength is that Whitford spends five to eight percent of our total sales in R&D, which is very rare in our industry," he explained. "As a result, every two to three years, we develop new products to meet market needs. That's how we create the opportunities for ourselves, instead of waiting for those opportunities to develop. For example, in 2016 we introduced five new coatings: two for premium cookware, two for premium bakeware, and one—Tetran—for rice cookers. The new Tetran coating has six times more extended release properties than conventional rice-cooker coating systems. So you can imagine how big the business potential in the rice-cooker market is for Whitford. We began a pilot program for Tetran with three customers in 2016."

The timing of the launch of the new Tetran coating could not have been better for the company. For decades, China's vast domestic rice-cooker market had been tied to very low-end models, but in 2016, an in-depth article appeared in the *Wall Street Journal* under the headline "The Rice Cooker Has Become a Test of China's Ability to Fix Its Economy": "With low-cost exports on the wane, the country is struggling to make high-quality goods for a rising middle class," it reported. "In a bid for new growth, China hopes to produce more high-end goods to sell domestically...For decades, China's economy blossomed through low-cost exports built on inexpensive labor. That era is coming to an end, because of rising wages, overproduction and competition from Vietnam and Bangladesh."[7]

Whitford operations in Asia address the consumer markets there, while also providing coatings for manufacturers that service markets throughout the world. While the company thereby

---

7 Te-Ping Chen, "The Rice Cooker Has Become a Test of China's Ability to Fix Its Economy," *Wall Street Journal*, August 3, 2016.

has the advantage of the breadth of this geographic diversification, it is subject to the economic instabilities of its various sectors: the years-long sluggishness of the European economy, which began in 2008, and the slowing of China's economic growth beginning in 2015.

"Whitford's business in Asia certainly ties in with what is going on elsewhere, since a large portion of our business is with manufacturers exporting their finished product to the rest of the world," Wong said. "Even when the worldwide market economy has not been stable, and/or the marketing mix is getting very complex and confused, Whitford's business in Asia remains promising."

Speaking for the Industry

In the David-and-Goliath history of Whitford versus DuPont, Whitford most often has chosen to take a more well-defined, tactical approach. However, if the company's emphasis on close, personal contact and addressing specific customer needs would consequently limit its range of prospects, Whitford has always been attentive to developments that would allow it to get in front of a much larger audience. Although the company had come later than DuPont to the business of nonstick coatings, Whitford nonetheless found opportunities to have an impact on how the industry in general defined itself.

When the nonstick business was just getting underway, tests had to be developed for dry-film lubrication to learn about such issues as adhesion, coefficient of friction, and temperature capabilities, as well as resistance to abrasion, chemicals, and ultraviolet light. While DuPont claimed to have such methodology, the company would not share it. Whitford developed its own battery of test methods, then took a different approach. The company documented the results and published them—then offered the document to the entire industry, all 126 pages of it.

When the engineering standards committee of the Cookware Manufacturers Association (CMA) decided to develop industry standard tests, it began with Whitford's test methods and procedures, which were adopted with few changes. This became one of many examples of how Whitford positioned itself as the industry's information source on nonstick coatings, further credentialing its product line for prospects and existing customers.

A Matter of Integrity

Gaining respect by working with customers on problem-solving...Repeatedly demonstrating that Whitford not only cares about its business but the success of the industry in general... Terms like "patience" and "persistence" frequently applied when describing how Whitford stays connected with customers. All descriptive of a policy of maintaining the highest levels of integrity in the way Whitford has always sought to gain and retain customers' trust. Never straying from consistency in product integrity is always a full-time job, applied across the board, no matter the attractiveness of short cuts or less expensive alternatives to best practices.

In her book *Dishes & Beverages of the Old South,* published at the turn of the twentieth century, the poet, essayist, and short-story writer Martha McCulloch-Williams wrote, "You will never get out of a pot or pan anything fundamentally better than what went into it." The author was talking about the importance of ingredients in a recipe, but the sentence translates seamlessly to a reference about nonstick coatings.

"You can make a black coating with carbon black," Dave Willis explained. "It's what's used to make tires. You can take that same carbon black and use it in a coating, except that it's not FDA acceptable. The carbon black for tires is one dollar a pound. The FDA-acceptable carbon black is eight dollars a pound. Some coating formulators use the dollar one. Is it going to kill anybody? Absolutely not. But if you are certifying that your products meet FDA rules, you better use the eight-dollar pigment."

There are many other examples of where coating manufacturers can cut corners.

"A number of acrylics are used as coalescing agents," Willis said. "Some are frankly not FDA-acceptable for cookware, but they are relatively inexpensive and are useful for other applications. We use the more expensive, FDA-acceptable acrylics on our cookware coatings, which means we will never have the least expensive formula."

Willis insisted this kind of attention to doing things correctly, even if that is more expensive, is the only way Whitford will ever conduct its business.

"That's important to our customers, and it is important to me as an individual," he said. "What we tell our customers is, 'If you get it from us, you will get it right.'"

CHAPTER 11

THINKING OUTSIDE THE BOX... OR NOT

> *While solving the problem, you will be encouraged to think aloud. When thinking aloud you should do the following: Say whatever's on your mind. Don't hold back hunches, guesses, wild ideas, images, plans or goals.*
> —"SOLVING THE NINE-DOT PROBLEM," WIKIPEDIA

When does thinking outside the box get you to thinking about the inside of the box as well, or the entire box itself as an entity? To wit, there is probably little reason to think about what role a slippery coating might play in packaging to help it hold up against the rigors of shipment...or is there? Pistons and seals in automobiles; nuts and bolts on oil rigs and windmills; cookware, bakeware, small appliances...but coating paper?

163

Dave Willis retrieved several sheets of paper from a cabinet behind him and placed them on his desk in front of a visitor—sheets of kraft paper coated with fluoropolymer. "According to some people, it can't be done with paper," he said. "But we don't have to put fluoropolymers just on metal. There is nothing that says we absolutely have to do it only that way. Of course, I get the argument that paper is not stable and that it has other problems."

Willis gestured at the coated paper. "Well," he continued, "this is not made to wrap hamburgers. This is a dense paper with a polymer coating, and it has a much heavier weight. Think about file folders or cardboard boxes. There are all manner of papers that are dimensionally stable."

All right, then, to vault really far afield, how else could you use polymer-coated paper?

"It would make a superb bearing," Willis said.

What? Those greasy machine parts that keep other parts in place in order to perform their designated functions? Paper? Even coated paper?

"Most people think of bearings as metal ball bearings and roller bearings," Willis went on. "What they don't realize is that there are millions—absolutely millions—of products called bearings that are really only positioning devices. They are used to keep a metal shaft off a metal housing. There is not much pressure, and many times they are used just to hold a moving object in place. Helicopters, for example, use such bearings to position some components. That's the sort of application that could benefit from the use of a fluoropolymer-coated paper bearing."

He insisted that sort of application is just scratching the surface for fluoropolymer-coated paper bearings.

"Other potential markets are just waiting for this type of product," he said. "Years ago, when I got started in this business, Whirlpool was using ninety thousand bearings a day in its manufacturing processes. The company was selling something like eighteen million machines, full of bearings just to hold things in place. Maybe they don't use that many bearings today, but it is an application that is definitely worth exploring."

Moving from Concept to Reality
The monologue about possibilities, no matter how seemingly far-fetched, is all part of an inquiring-mind syndrome that has been an infectious disease at Whitford since the very beginning, spreading throughout the company ever since. Definitely not fatal—in fact, energizing. Therefore, it's not surprising that something began to stir with Whirlpool.

"We have interest from Whirlpool for one application: crisper drawer slides," said Spencer Siegel, who is responsible for the company's sales efforts for paper. "With samples in hand, I can target furniture drawer slides as well. I also pursue markets where plastic bearings or oils and greases are currently used. In the case of the former, the advantage would be a direct cost savings. In the case of the latter, the savings would be realized in reduced or eliminated maintenance."

As for the more traditional concept of paper and cardboard, there is a great potential for business from companies both large and small, especially given all the online orders that require shipments coming from all over the world.

"Kodak ships painted printer cabinets from Asia that arrive with the paint damaged because the cardboard or other packaging products rub against the surfaces," Siegel said. "The company wants a PTFE-coated paper disk, with adhesive on the opposite side, so they can peel and stick it onto any surface that touches their product in order to protect it during transit. In this case, the coated paper would contact the painted surfaces and provide a smooth, low-friction interface."

The textiles industry is another of Siegel's seemingly unlikely targets: coatings for high-performance ropes and cordage, automobile belts, conveyor belts, cargo netting, outdoor furnishings, seating fabrics, and luggage fabrics. The coatings bring an assortment of performance enhancements, including improved comfort, extended life expectancy, reduced energy consumption, and other characteristics depending on the particular requirements of the application.

Whitford chemists have created a product category called EterniTex, a broad range of high-performance liquids for application to natural and synthetic fibers used with woven and nonwoven fabrics. They provide a combination of strength and flexibility, improve the durability of the fabrics, and extend their life expectancy through increased abrasion resistance and friction reduction. These EterniTex products are frequently customized for an intended application, so they can also impart a combination of attributes to provide an improved final product.

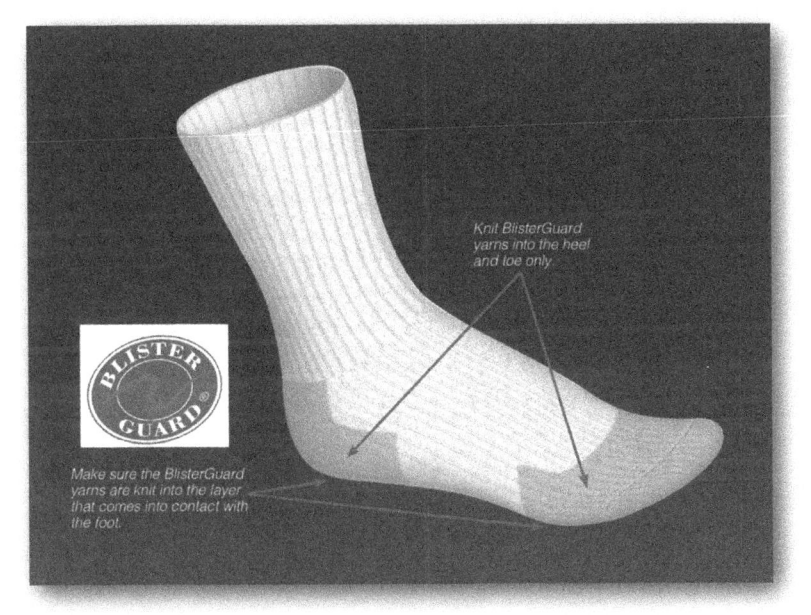

Socks, knitted with pretreated Blisterguard yarns, reduce blisters.

Then there is nonstick coating for athletic socks. Athletic socks? The name of the relevant coating, Whitford's trademarked BlisterGuard, provides a none-too-subtle clue as to where the discussion is headed. Whether running a road race or darting around a soccer field, hiking in the high country or walking in a picturesque European village, painful blisters can take the fun out of the pursuit. Socks knitted with pretreated BlisterGuard yarns in the heel and toe have reduced friction, heat buildup, blistering, and chafing.

As with other Whitford businesses, the company's textiles business is customer and market driven. Products previously developed in this part of the business that did not find commercial homes may actually find one or more.

"I consider already existing products, plus new technologies, as I find unmet needs in the markets I've been researching and pursuing," Siegel said.

A Major Commitment to Medical

Medical coatings, a new market for Whitford.

In a spanking new, completely renovated area at the Whitford headquarters and manufacturing facility in Elverson, Pennsylvania, are the offices of the medical coatings group. Investment in the new facility included equipment specific to the requirements of medical device manufacturers, as well as a separate quality-control laboratory. It also required hiring management and operations personnel specifically to address this aspect of Whitford's business. The bright new offices are apart from the bustle of the building's other manufacturing areas and convey the feeling of a new wing at a hospital.

"And it's quiet," said Darlee Burns, industry manager, medical device coatings. "That allows us to get a great deal of work done in a short amount of time, because there are fewer interruptions. This is imperative, as there are huge amounts of work to be done and high expectations of the team."

An important element in establishing those credentials is the experience and expertise of the personnel themselves. Burns, for example, spent fifteen years in the medical device and molecular diagnostics industries on the quality and operations side of the business and in analytical development as well, giving her an edge when making strategic decisions regarding the business. Also critical to Whitford's medical coatings group is certification by the International Organization for Standardization, based in Geneva, Switzerland, a designation the company received in December 2015.

"This ISO 13485 certification reassures customers when ordering Whitford coatings," explained Charlie Fields, global business manager, medical device coatings. "Whether the products are catheter guide wires, scalpel blades, or other devices that benefit from a PTFE, FEP, or other fluoropolymer coating, customers know that this coating is reproducible, and they will receive the same formula every single time. This guarantee is vital with medical coatings. It's important to note that all of our processes are reviewed on a regular basis. ISO 13485 tells customers that we will be a strong, reliable link in their supply chain, able to support them with documentation above and beyond what ISO requires."

The ISO certification adds value to the entire product portfolio of Whitford's medical coatings group. While Whitford invested a large amount of time and money into building its new, dedicated medical facility, additional time was invested in standardizing and documenting processes in order to be certified. As a result, customers are now able to save time and money by eliminating certain steps from their supplier search process.

"Customers know that we have been audited to the full ISO extent, and they no longer need to invest their own time into an additional audit," Fields said. "Many of them will be able to set us up as a critical supplier due to the quality system certificate that we now possess. Customers can trust that we will provide support should they decide to submit to the FDA. Overall, ISO 13485 improves the customer experience and ensures that the Whitford medical coatings group continuously works to improve our products and process."

An ability to concentrate on the challenges at hand, with the fewest possible distractions, is paramount when building a new business in high-performance fluoropolymer coatings on medical devices in order to take on the already-established competition. Nonetheless, fluoropolymer coatings have been successfully used on medical devices for many years, offering a variety of important benefits, and Whitford has a long tradition of taking on established competition in other business genres. A logical starting point, however, was repositioning some existing business.

"The initial push has been to convert current customers from ordering our industrial material to the dedicated material made in the medical coatings facility," Burns explained. "Then we focus on new business generation. Our aim is to become a global leader in medical-coating supply. Having a dedicated facility reinforces our policy of providing exceptional quality and security of supply, at a time when many other coating manufacturers are struggling to meet the rising regulatory demands of the medical industry."

While Whitford offers a similar replacement version of a competitor's principal product, the company also supports other chemistries that the competition doesn't, not only in products other companies lack, but in a range of colors for each product family.

The group serves coating-applications companies that are contracted by large medical original equipment manufacturers, as well as the OEMs themselves.

"The goal is to have our coatings specified by the OEM," Burns said. "Then, whether they apply or contract the application process out, we will still gain the business. The challenge lies in ensuring these companies know that we understand the medical device market, we know the documentation and level of manufacturing excellence they require, and are not just a commodity supplier anymore. We are building in value to the supply chain, and sometimes that can be an abstract concept."

"Making medical coatings is a different world for sure," she said, "but making product and supporting customers is a universal business strategy."

Adding Epoxy to the Mix

In mid-2004, Whitford purchased Polymeric Systems, Inc., a leader in the development and manufacture of high-performance sealants, caulks, and epoxy adhesives. PSI formulations are found in a wide range of industrial, commercial, and do-it-yourself applications and are available with special performance properties for many unique applications. The company is a private label and toll manufacturer, developing products for many large adhesive and sealant companies.

As a toll manufacturer, PSI has nondisclosure agreements with the companies with which it does business. Many companies utilize this service and these products to complete their brand product lines. When companies need a certain product to do a particular job but don't have the manufacturing or packaging space, let alone the technology to develop and manufacture such products, PSI steps into the void, offering solutions that undergo the same careful QC, manufacturing, and packaging processes as PSI-branded products.

Since its founding in 1969, PSI has been application oriented, focused on supplying custom products for special requirements, while at the same time emphasizing the development of environmentally friendly answers for its customers.

Ted Flint, a chemical engineering graduate of Villanova University, launched PSI in a small, rented building in Pottstown, Pennsylvania. Initially, it was a one-man, one-woman operation, Ted handling product development, production, and sales, while his wife, Debby, kept the books and delivered finished goods. The business grew but was limited in scope because of the lack of product diversity. Then in 1972 came its first breakthrough.

Not unlike the challenges confronting Whitford's first chemist in the earliest days of Whitford Chemical, Flint faced chemical conundrums if he wanted to build PSI's business. He had toyed with epoxy adhesives but was frustrated by the messy, wasteful way they were applied. The epoxy resin and curing agent/hardener had to be kept apart until ready for use. Then they were scooped out onto a surface and stirred together with a disposable tool, often hardening too quickly. Sometimes, due to this inefficiency, the two ingredients weren't mixed in precisely equal amounts, reducing adhesion.

Flint was convinced he needed to eliminate the waste and simplify the mixing procedure by combining the two ingredients into one easy-to-use product. His ingenious solution was side-by-side extruded putty ribbons or strips of the two parts, each sandwiched between protective plastic. This would allow the user simply to cut off equal amounts of the two strips, remove the plastic, and knead the two ingredients together until they formed a uniform color. PSI's first product, appropriately called Kneadatite epoxy putty tape, was blue (for the epoxy) and yellow (for the hardener), which formed a green epoxy repair putty when completely mixed.

Kneadatite could be formed like modeling clay to sculpt, build up, or wrap any object. After several hours, it hardened and was remarkably resistant to chemicals, temperature extremes, and shattering. Production began in 1972, and in 1973 Flint received the first of several patents for epoxy putties. Kneadatite remains one of PSI's best sellers.

Encouraged by his success with Kneadatite, Flint then sought to develop faster-curing repair epoxies. But the original Kneadatite ribbon form adversely affected the new, faster hardener with which he was experimenting by permitting too much exposure to air. Again, a unique packaging solution provided an answer: an inner cylinder of hardener wrapped with an outer cylinder of epoxy, like one Tootsie Roll wrapped around another. While there was surface to surface contact, no chemical reaction took place. The faster hardener, which went bad if exposed to air, was protected by the outer layer of epoxy.

The user simply cuts off as much as he or she wanted, providing the perfect amount of each ingredient. As with Kneadatite, the different-colored ingredients were kneaded together until they reached a consistent color, indicating they were ready for application.

Kneadatite is available in eight variations for specific needs.

Using this technology, a whole line of application-specific epoxy putties was developed for the repair of wood, steel, concrete, aluminum, copper, plastic, and fiberglass, as well as a general-purpose repair putty. The fiberglass version actually cures underwater, and the wood version floats. As business flourished, PSI moved three times, each time into a larger facility.

In 2003, having run their company for thirty-four years, the Flints pulled back from the day-to-day business and began serious discussions with potential buyers. Running the business in their place was Debbie Parkes, whom they had hired in 2002 and promoted to vice president and general manager in 2003. Parkes had spent the first five years of her business career in the finance department at Hewlett-Packard in Colorado, then more than twenty years as vice president of her family's business in Philadelphia, designing and manufacturing industrial drying equipment.

"When Whitford acquired PSI in 2004, Dave Willis gave me the opportunity to continue in the role of managing director of PSI," Parkes said. "In fact, Dave kept on the entire PSI team after the acquisition, welcoming everyone into the Whitford family. He also gave us the ability to purchase equipment and expand the business in ways that were not possible before. He believed in reinvesting in and growing all of his companies, even if it meant taking calculated risks. PSI was no exception. Today, we can offer more and better products to our customers—more than five hundred customers and hundreds of products—and the possibilities continue."

PSI has worked on joint projects with Whitford over the years, with both companies' sales and technical people working hand in hand to help find solutions to the problems of their respective customers. They also share sales resources around the world to promote and sell each other's products.

Environmentally Friendly Products

PSI's manufacturing processes are designed to comply with the strictest of government environmental regulations. From its very beginning, protecting the environment has been an integral part of the company's product-development objectives. Most of its product formulations are completely free of solvents, toxic chemicals, and volatile organic compounds (VOCs). This makes them user friendly and avoids any contamination to the environment. The company is the industry's leading formulator of low-VOC, nonhazardous modified silane-, silicone-, and polymer-based products.

In addition to its attention to the environmental impact of its own products, part of PSI's manufacturing process includes examination of various packaging types to determine how best to protect the product during transit and storage, yet add only the minimal amount to the waste stream at the consumer's end. PSI also has a plant-wide waste-reduction program that is regularly examined to reduce the waste stream from office and manufacturing operations.

Innovation Above and Beyond

Operating within a corporate mind-set that promotes innovation and exploration can create forays into related areas outside the lines of the company's day-to-day business. Case in point: roller coating of discs for cookware has been in use for a long time. It is almost 100 percent efficient, wasting very little coating material. However, the appearance and quality level of a roller-coated product are poor. A sprayed product, on the other hand, has a very smooth, attractive-looking finish. However, the spray process is only about 60 percent efficient on a good day—that is, it wastes at least 40 percent of the coating material in overspray. Not so for a curtain coater, which is used to apply coating to flat blanks that then are heat-cured and pressed into cookware. Curtain coating was considered the Holy Grail of application methods because it would combine the smooth finish of a spray coat with the efficiency of a roller coat. But…

"Before Whitford, this had never been done successfully with a nonstick coating for cookware," explained John Russo, Whitford's very hands-on lab manager. "Every aspect of the process is difficult for a thin-film application of fluoropolymer coatings. The coatings were not designed to take the kind of abuse they receive by being pumped through a curtain coater, and the machines were not designed to run this type of material."

Curtain coating was mainly used in the wood industry for processes such as applying the glue that holds plywood sheets together. There, appearance was not an issue, control was loose, and the goal was to put down a heavy film. Any attempts by Whitford to apply this methodology to nonstick coatings would need to find a way to make it work for coatings being applied at less than 0.02 inch and to make the resulting look free of imperfections. Not a challenge that would stop Russo and his colleagues.

The curtain coater, one of Whitford's many innovations in coating technology.

"We would need to modify additives and defoamers in our coatings," he said, "but the biggest challenge was modifying the pumping system to work with the coatings. So even though other companies manufactured the curtain-coater machines, we had to modify them before anyone could run nonstick coatings. It was a matter of semi-educated engineering of different setups until we could get it to work."

To do that meant Russo and his team traveling and hauling components hither and yon.

"All the production scale-up trials were run in Italy," he said, "so we spent a lot of time there, going back and forth before things worked. On some of those trips, we carried large numbers of parts to modify the curtain machine for better results. Looking back, we really took the scenic route to success with this project, but Whitford never gave up, and our innovations succeeded where none had before."

If there is a downside to what the Whitford team accomplished with these modifications, it can be said they were too successful. The output of the coated parts is so fast, many applicators simply do not have the production capability to keep pace.

"It was a win to make this happen," Russo said, "but in the end, there were variables that stopped people from buying in. The biggest being unless they already did roller coating, they did not have ovens that could keep up with the coating, so it would mean more than $1 million in investments over and above the curtain machine costs."

The Ongoing Commitment to Explore
The whole curtain-coater exercise begs a question: Wouldn't working to redesign machines to save more than 40 percent of

the material in a coating process be somewhat counterproductive for Whitford, since it would cause customers to use that much less of its product?

"Absolutely," Russo answered. "We knew we were going to sell less coating, but it was viewed as such an advantage to the customer that it would ensure we would have the business, and the competition would not."

Whitford has long prided itself on promoting different approaches to sales and marketing, always with the objective of producing a better outcome. Demonstrating to customers how to build a machine that will cause them to use *less* of Whitford's product is simply another example of the company's commitment to improving how its industry defines its business. If they say it can't be done, Whitford people will explore how to do it. And even if that process sometimes produces an outcome for which a need has yet to develop, the company's history has demonstrated time and again that a need will eventually catch up to and connect with the solution.

Stagnation has never been part of the Whitford way, resting on the laurels of past successes never part of the corporate mindset. If the game of rock-paper-scissors can be looked on as a metaphor for the competitive business world, Whitford can say it is already coating paper and medical scissors, but if anyone insists that there really is no good reason to coat a rock, well…there's that "it-can't-be-done" negativity again.

Hmm.

CHAPTER 12

DEVELOPING A DIFFERENT BUSINESS APPROACH

> *Regardless of which path customers take, or in which order they take them, they want to deal with people who can help them move toward a purchase decision... In fact, B2B buyers report that, compared to other sources of information, these interactions are the most influential in their decision making process.*
> —FRANK V. CESPEDES AND TIFFANI BOVA, HARVARD BUSINESS REVIEW, AUGUST 5, 2015

The company that eventually grew into Whitford Worldwide began as a classic start-up, slowly, with just $2,000 in sales closing out its first two months in existence at the end of 1969. For the company's first full year in 1970, sales were better—a grand total of $95,000—but still very wobbly, even by a mid-1960s yardstick. During this time, Ted Rehmeyer, Dave Willis's cofounding partner, went back to the Wharton School of Business at the University of Pennsylvania to pursue an MBA in production management.

As part of the course, a team was put together to study a company and make recommendations to its management as to what they could do to boost the business. Rehmeyer asked if Willis had any objection to a visit and an analysis. Willis agreed.

"We could use all the help we could get," he recalled. "Four or five of Ted's fellow students came out to our small building on the same site as our chemicals business. We spent some time explaining what we did and some of the theory behind the products. Basically, we led them through our entire business."

The Wharton team went away, completed their analysis, then returned with their recommendation.

"Their report and ultimate suggestion would today be called 'pump and dump,'" Willis said. "That is, get all the sales possible, as soon as possible, even at low selling prices, and then sell the company and go do something else. Some fifty years later, we are still giving that recommendation all the consideration it deserves."

It's not surprising there are not a lot of MBAs at Whitford. Only two that Willis said he was aware of. "Or only two who will admit to it," he added with a smile.

This is not to say there are no lessons one can take from a business school education. Willis, after all, was also a graduate of Wharton. But from the outset, he was determined to start a business that addressed the needs of the real world, a business that made things, would continue to make those things better and better, and would grow the business as a result. He was not interested in pump-and-dump schemes or wheeling and dealing just to pile up wealth. Success would not be via some imposed business model or approach; Whitford would develop its own business approach as it went along.

Taking the Show on the Road

At the core of that approach were face-to-face sales calls. That would seem a logical place to start to build a business in the pre-Internet days of the late '60s and early '70s. It became apparent from the outset, however, that what business planners and essayists in the Internet era would eventually christen "outside sales" were simply good old tried-and-true sales calls, and they would remain firmly established *inside* the Whitford playbook.

Whitford's first coating was barely out of the chem lab when Willis had the ear of a friend at Xomox Corporation. At a face to face over breakfast in a diner, Willis laid out a compelling case to try the newly developed Xylan 1010 on a sticking valve problem Xomox could not seem to solve. It worked, and Whitford sold Xomox a whopping five gallons of the Xylan. It was a start, however, and a demonstration that Xylan worked for real-world applications.

From his days of rounding up business far and wide when he was sales manager at LNP (see chapter two), Willis knew Whitford would need to take its show on the road. So, using a list of coating applicators published by DuPont and armed with an exciting new product, Willis and his lone salesman at the time divvied up the country and went out on sales calls.

"We had virtually nothing but the published list of DuPont industrial applicators," Willis recalled, "which included names and addresses of their largest and most attractive accounts. It was an obvious place to start."

After establishing some rapport with the DuPont applicators he visited, Willis continued to hone his approach. He asked pointed questions. Where are you having problems with the coatings you're using? Are they living up to your expectations? What improvements would you make if you were designing the ideal coating?

"Eventually, I'd ask who their competitors were, which was the beginning of an extended prospect list," he said. "I also suggested that we make joint sales calls, enabling the applicator to sell its services and me to sell the coatings."

Additional Benefits of the Sit-Down

Throughout any discussion of Whitford's approach to business, the issue of sitting down with a customer or prospect to discuss specific solutions to specific issues comes up repeatedly. But how—specifically—does that work?

Before joining Whitford's consumer marketing team, Jim Gibian worked for a company called Lifetime Brands, a large owner and licensor of housewares brands. Therefore, he had experience on both sides of the customer-seller relationship.

"At Lifetime Brands, I was responsible for product development and marketing for cookware and bakeware," he said, "so I got to know Whitford. The Whitford people I dealt with took an inordinate amount of time to learn about a customer's business, and they were doing an incredibly good job at matching needs to a coating."

In addition to a fairly straightforward match of a cookware or bakeware product to a coating, however, sometimes the process of marrying the two could go well beyond that. That, for Gibian, was one of the areas that set Whitford apart from the competition.

"The design of a product can determine the performance needed from a coating," he explained, "but the reverse can also be true. The use of a coating can impact *how* you design the product. Often, we were talking about the design materials to make sure the coating could be applied properly. So there is a lot of involvement between Whitford and brand owners, retailers, importers, and manufacturers. As a result, I spent a lot of time with Whitford, together developing an understanding of what I needed. That relationship went on for almost ten years."

The closeness of the relationship eventually led to Gibian's joining Whitford to help with the marketing on the consumer side, bringing with him all the advantages of his experience on the other side of the equation.

"It's amazing when you are on this side, and you understand what lengths Whitford goes through to satisfy the demands of a brand owner," he said. "Sometimes, the brand owner's knowledge can be limited, i.e., the coating has to be nonstick, it has to work for its intended purpose, and it can't have any problems with food safety. In order to achieve that, however, there is a lot that goes on behind the curtain. I like to use the analogy of the

Wizard of Oz. Whitford is behind the curtain pushing and pulling all the levers, and when that curtain opens, it's astounding what's on that piece of cookware or bakeware. It's incredible the science and technology used to determine that. But you need to be able to explain this to people who are not chemists."

Coatings Education at Whitford University

Creating informed customers has been an ongoing effort at Whitford for decades. In 1990, the company decided to formalize a program to share what it had learned with its customers. It founded "Whitford University," a training program held several times a year in a number of its offices around the world.

With turnover and growth, Whitford's customers are continually hiring new people, many of whom are novices in the rather complicated business of handling and applying high-performance coatings. Furthermore, there is surprisingly little formal training available related to the technology. Customers becoming knowledgeable in the technology and how to apply the coatings is important to Whitford's developing ongoing relationships with them.

The training programs at WU last several days and combine classroom lectures with practical exercises in the laboratory. Lectures cover such subjects as types of coatings, product testing, quality control, surface preparation, and environmental regulations. Laboratory work includes familiarization with all types of application equipment and techniques, color matching, troubleshooting typical problems, and demonstrations of testing equipment. The classes are kept small, usually twenty to twenty-five people.

Kurt Mecray teaching at Whitford University. Inset of the certificate awarded at the end of the session.

US sessions are held at Whitford headquarters in Elverson, Pennsylvania, attracting attendees mostly from the Western Hemisphere. Sessions in the United Kingdom draw attendees from across Europe. Participants in the China sessions are drawn from throughout Asia. Since its inception, the program has attracted several thousand attendees from more than forty countries.

While the courses are designed to add to the knowledge base of Whitford's customers, Whitford benefits as well. Company managers who conduct the courses get to hear candid, focused questions from their target audience. This creates a better understanding of customers' problems, which can identify solutions, and those solutions may well include a Whitford coating. It also provides an opportunity to show how Whitford's R&D might help customers with projects in the planning stages.

"The programs work particularly well for customers' new employees," explained Mike Miller, former chief operating officer and the person most responsible for the creation and development of the program. "Those usually are the people out in the factory with spray guns and perhaps unfamiliar with our products or how to apply them. The programs establish us as *the* company that knows the most about coatings. In fact, we're unaware of any competitor that offers such training."

The training establishes strong personal relationships, since real faces and personalities replace whatever vague images attendees may have had of Whitford, while learning how to solve problems that occur on their factory floors makes them less likely to call Whitford and ask to be bailed out of a situation.

Mike Miller lecturing in the Whitford "War Room."

"These classes are not conducted without some enlightened self-interest," Miller said. "At the end of the program, we give people a CD containing all the lectures they have seen, including the handouts and printed materials. They go away wiser than when they came in. And feeling privileged. They become the knowledgeable, go-to people at their companies concerning Whitford and our products. And, of course, we have set up lines of communication that can be invaluable for years to come."

A Place for Inside Sales
All the emphasis on interacting with customers face to face does not eliminate the need for an inside-sales effort, especially in the age of Internet obsessiveness. For Whitford, however, to work inside sales requires understanding how the outside-sales effort works, as opposed to hiring salespeople who spend their entire corporate existence in front of a computer.

Dave Willis's son, Brian, who heads the inside-sales efforts, had literally grown up in the family business. Starting as a fifteen-year old, he worked in production during summer breaks in high school.

"In 1978, I came on board full time," he said. "After four years in college, I'd had enough and was out of money. At that point, Dad moved the company to a new facility, which I helped design and build, and did it without losing a day in production."

When business began picking up in the Oil Patch, the company needed somebody in Houston. Brian was tapped for the assignment. A background in engineering became a valuable asset.

"I didn't think I was a sales guy at all, let alone selling coatings in Houston to the oil and gas industry," he said. "But I found that traditional sales guys weren't really accepted there. Technical guys fit in. So in 1982, I moved to Houston. I was also covering western territories and finally all territory west of the Mississippi."

After traveling for twenty-five years, Willis decided he needed a change.

"So I've been doing inside sales for the last ten years," he said. "I understand all the nuances and intricacies of applications, but 'outside,' I was being used to do routine customer calls. So working this way with engineers 'inside,' I'm also really selling. Before I started this job, we had about a hundred and fifty specifications listed; now we're up to four hundred."

Beyond the Immediate Business Relationship

While paying close attention when a customer or prospective customer is talking about product requirements is at the core of the Whitford sales process, really listening can rise to a higher level of attention. That high art of listening involves attentiveness even when it is not directly part of a sales effort. And that sort of attention has cemented relationships for Whitford that have been solid for decades.

For example, Tramontina USA is part of a large Brazilian enterprise that markets cookware in the United States. When the company was evaluating how to increase production in the United States, Dave Willis suggested that Antonio Galafassi, the president, consider buying a large, recently deserted Mirro

Cookware plant in Manitowoc, Wisconsin. Willis was convinced this would be a really important move for Tramontina, since the Wisconsin factory was empty, should be inexpensive to buy, and was surrounded by a fully trained labor force that was out of work. It took some convincing, but Tramontina did buy the factory, and having that production capability evolved into a huge success.

"I'll never forget that you practically put us in the cookware business many years ago, when you saw the opportunity for us to take over the Mirro plant," Galafassi wrote Willis. "At first, I second-guessed you. But your encouragement made me open my eyes and see the opportunity ahead of us. I can honestly say it was probably the best business venture in which I have ever engaged. In a special way, and I say this from my heart, you were a real inspiration, like a few other special people, in the making of the 'Tramontina Made in the USA.' Believe me, this is paying big dividends for business and brand recognition. Today, I want you to feel proud of being part of Tramontina as a special friend of the house, key vendor, and instrumental in the battles to make the Tramontina Made in USA a success story."

Persistence Personified

The undercurrent of persistence that runs throughout the Whitford business approach involves continuous attention mentally and the expenditure of a good deal of energy. The result of the approach is many, many customers scattered throughout the world—in effect, lots of relatively small customers. No one customer represents more than about 2.5 percent to 3 percent of total sales. Think of it as a very well-diversified portfolio.

So if dependence on a handful of godfather clients creates a vulnerability, Whitford's diversified customer base is the antidote to that vulnerability, a vindication of all the client servicing involved in the Whitford business approach.

"You are naïve or spending too much time on your smartphone if you believe that a combination of economics, solution identification, product application, risk management, and political journey through the buyer's organization is now handled predominately online in most buying scenarios without knowledgeable and savvy sales help," Frank V. Cespedes and Tiffani Bova wrote in *Harvard Business Review*. "Buying is a continuous and dynamic process...Salespeople are not disappearing."[8]

They are not disappearing. They work for Whitford and are on the road, tending to their existing customers and/or generating new business.

---

8 Frank V. Cespedes and Tiffani Bova, "The Most Influential B2B Marketing Activities," *Harvard Business Review*, August 5, 2015.

CHAPTER 13

CREATING AND BUILDING A CONSISTENT BRAND IDENTITY

> *The aim of marketing is to know and understand the customer so well the product or service fits...and sells itself.*
> —PETER DRUCKER

Sales without marketing is akin to fighting your battles without a war plan. Advertising, direct mail, various forms of promotion, and media-relations efforts, all coalescing to create an awareness of the company's brand, not only play a vital role in setting the table for a sales force to move in and close deals but play the equally vital role of helping to define the company.

If Whitford Corporation was to have a corporate existence of any longevity, a series of punchy direct-mail pieces in the very beginning would be simply that: a beginning. (See chapter four.) Everything the company did in the way of marketing would need to support a consistent brand image. While instituting a clever direct-mail campaign to make potential customers aware of the new company's existence, Tony Weir, the company's marketing guru at the outset, was at the same time committed to building the Whitford brand.

Thus began a business relationship of more than forty-five years, first with Weir operating outside the company, then in 1990, as sales climbed toward $20 million and the prospect of a six-figure pretax profit, he joined Whitford full time. With Weir assuming the management of Whitford's marketing communications on a worldwide basis, Whitford had, in effect, the benefit of a full-fledged advertising agency in house.

As much as Willis's focus was on selling, Weir was equally focused on branding.

"Corporations and brands are not much different from individual people," he explained. "Those who are most memorable are generally those who are distinctive in their appearance and performance and are consistent, so that over time, they come to be known for and identified by their 'brand personality.'"

While it would appear, initially, that going up against a competitor the size of DuPont could ultimately crush a much-smaller rival, if you examined the situation closely, looking for DuPont's vulnerabilities and Whitford's assets, you could devise an effective marketing strategy. Weir's work at Ogilvy & Mather and his appreciation for successful advertising programs across a wide spectrum of industries had prepared him to provide exactly the kind of assistance Whitford needed.

"We were offering a secondary product," he explained. "The ultimate consumer buys fry pans, not nonstick coatings, and we had neither the marketing muscle nor the financial wherewithal of DuPont. DuPont created the category and spent hundreds of millions of dollars educating the general public about nonstick coatings—for which we are most grateful. We decided to invest our meager funds in advertising to those in a position to specify the coatings used, whether on cookware and bakeware, deep-sea oil rigs, automobiles, roofing fasteners, tire molds, wherever. And we have never wavered."

A Matter of Differentiating

Weir felt that to be effective, Whitford's marketing was a matter of differentiating. From the very beginning, he felt it was obvious that Whitford needed a meaningful point of difference to separate it from DuPont. After all, DuPont had launched the nonstick category and dominated the market. It would be impossible to go head-to-head with its advertising budget, market power, or deep pockets. Whitford simply could not compete on the same terms. While Whitford needed to differentiate, it also needed to take a path DuPont would be unlikely to follow.

Weir liked Whitford's approach of customizing its products. It could form the basis of competing with DuPont, and he put that into words: "Whitford's not in the business of selling products. We're in the business of solving problems for our customers. So long as we remember this, the selling of our products will take care of itself."

The customization approach further encouraged a large and growing number of active formulae, as Whitford's tailor-made coatings proliferated, while DuPont had a limited number of coatings on the shelf, far fewer than Whitford offered. So Weir created the company's first corporate slogan/tagline: *Whitford: Makers of the largest, most complete line of fluoropolymer coatings in the world.*

Given that total Whitford's sales, in the early days, were little more than a rounding error compared to those of DuPont, the slogan may have been a bit brash. Nevertheless, it captured the essence of Whitford's focus on solving problems rather than just selling coatings.

Whitford's competitors often did not have a product that addressed a customer's precise needs. Therefore, the customer had to make do with a product that came close. Whitford, on the other hand, was willing to take what comes close and modify it to address a customer's specific need. While that was a boon to the sales department, it did not make it easy for the laboratory or manufacturing operations. DuPont may have had to contend with keeping approximately fifty products in its arsenal, but meeting Whitford's customers' needs resulted in a library of more than five thousand products in its line.

Further, Whitford innovations often included ancillary benefits that went beyond the useful properties of the coatings themselves. For example, if a coating could be applied at a significantly lower cure temperature, it would provide the customer substantial cost savings. Again, this made impressive fodder for direct mail.

"It reduces the cost of curing an average of 25 percent...If you're running a cure line five days a week, Friday is free...If you're running five production lines, you can close one of them without reducing throughput."

Birth of a Long-Standing Corporate Philosophy
The problem-/specific-solution approach became the basis of a philosophy that focused the company's efforts on something that

happens before the sale of a coating. By the mid-1970s, Whitford was actively promoting its commitment to this philosophy via ads in the trade press that addressed its markets. The ads emphasized that Whitford's was a commitment to serve customers better than anyone else in the market. The ads included a bounce-back coupon for prospects to provide contact information.

Then the company extended the shelf life of the ads, via its tried-and-true direct-mail program. The letters accompanying a copy of one of the ads read, in part: "When we say 'anyone,' in the market, we mean 'everyone'—including you-know-who-Pont. Call the two of us. Give each of us your problem. We both offer solutions. But we bet that ours will be more custom-tailored to your needs. And we bet you'll get it sooner. With a bet like that, how can you lose?"

This approach also reinforced the company's emphasis on customer service, which in turn led to the creation of research and development facilities far more extensive than Whitford's sales would have justified. That led to R&D in which the exploratory became commonplace. The lab continued to develop a string of new and improved products, creating a multiplier effect that brought in new customers.

Today, Whitford commits one of the highest percentages of company sales to R&D in the entire coatings industry. The company employs more than one hundred people worldwide to maintain R&D centers at each of its manufacturing facilities. As a result, the Whitford product line has become so expansive the company also offers coatings that have no fluoropolymers in them.

"While our tagline had always been 'Makers of the world's largest, most complete line of fluoropolymer coatings'—and that certainly remains true," Weir said, "Whitford is more than that today. So we changed our corporate tagline to 'Whitford, where good ideas come to the surface.'"

Hell's Kitchens

With the agility of an in-house advertising agency, Whitford has been in a position to act and/or react to competitive challenges quickly, in at least one instance turning a DuPont idea against it. In 1995, Whitford picked up news from the trade press that DuPont was planning an advertising campaign for its Teflon brand based on the endorsement of special chefs at high-end bed-and-breakfasts and restaurants in the New England area. The press reported that pans with an improved Teflon product had been placed with the chefs who, assuming satisfaction with the coating, would then provide endorsements that would be featured in advertising, most likely including recipes from the chefs.

"We decided we'd take a similar but opposite tack," Weir explained, "featuring our top-of-the-line coating, at that time called Excalibur, a nonstick applied over a matrix of stainless-steel 'peaks' and 'valleys' sprayed onto the surface of pots and pans, providing a strong, reinforced bed over and into which the coating is applied, locking it in place. The slogan for Excalibur was 'The toughest, longest-lasting, most durable nonstick coating system in the world.'"

But instead of using Belgian and French chefs at high-end restaurants, the Whitford approach was to find bottom-end greasy spoons, where it would be obvious that the cooks would be most likely to abuse any cookware they got their hands on. Whitford called the campaign "Hell's Kitchens."

One of the Hell's Kitchen campaign ads.

"About a mile from our office, then in Frazer, Pennsylvania, was a joint next to a bowling alley called the Alley Pub, where many of us ate lunch," Weir said. "It had a rough cement floor, old wooden booths with worn, red plastic seats and was run by Tressy Panzram, a tough lady who could handle, with one hand, any drunk who got out of line. We interviewed her, took some photos, and got permission to use her in an advertisement."

The headline of the ad, under a picture of Panzram holding a well-used, Excalibur-coated fry pan, quoted her saying, "The only thing in the Alley Pub tough enough to stand up to me is Excalibur. That's why I love it!"

Whitford quickly rounded up more such hash houses across the country, got their permission, interviewed the chefs, and took photos. The first ad began running in the trade press by July of that same year, about three months after the idea was hatched, which included two months of constant use of the coated cookware by each restaurant to test the Excalibur coating on the pans.

"We ran the campaign for more than a year," Weir said. "The DuPont high-end Teflon campaign never appeared, and we never heard another thing about it. We can't be sure 'Hell's Kitchens' killed it, but we like to think it did!"

Advertising in Trade Media

Expanding its efforts to use the most efficient ways of reaching its highly selective audience, Whitford began a limited advertising program in trade media in 1973. The company ran an ad about coating Clairol's Crazy Curl wands in *Housewares* magazine, the predecessor to *HomeWorld Business,* the industry's leading publication. Once again, the company's in-house agency provided the wherewithal to take advantage of unique opportunities.

"Whitford's media advertising in the United States focuses on one publication that reaches the consumer target markets with remarkable efficiency," explained Joan Eberhardt, the company's chief administrative officer. "We have an arrangement with the publication that if just prior to press time, it has an empty page it has not sold, we'll buy it—but at a generous discount.

This happens from time to time, and we can literally get the offering of an empty page in the morning and before the end of the day have written and produced a finished advertisement that is sent to the publication electronically."

Efforts such as these provide vital support to the retail sales team.

"In the retail department at Whitford, we don't sell a thing," explained Fran Groesbeck, who heads the company's retail marketing program. "We provide services, support, and free testing. It is a service program that ultimately makes great connections with those companies that use our coatings."

Dave Palcek, president and co-publisher, and Peter Giannetti, editor-in-chief, of "HomeWorld Business."

Although the end users don't buy from Whitford directly, they could turn to their factories and demand, "We want QuanTanium or Eclipse coatings."

"We call that 'pull' marketing," Groesbeck said. "Selling is pushing the factory, but this is pulling it through the factory."

Once again, Weir and his team directed these efforts in house.

"Our initial advertising was 'pushing' the specifiers to select our coatings for the products they intended to make and market," Weir explained. "As we grew, we decided to address the retail trade to 'pull' our coatings by helping retailers understand the differences among nonstick and decorative coatings, to incline them to ask for ours when talking with the manufacturers and marketers from whom they purchase product."

Whitford employs this pull marketing only on the consumer side.

"In the industrial world, where there is generally a greater depth of technical knowledge and experience with fluoropolymer coatings, the marketing communications program is more direct and limited," Weir said. "In addition, the logos and brand names, while important, are of less importance than on the consumer side and get less visibility. They are virtually never seen by the ultimate user of a tire mold, or a stud bolt, or an O-ring, for example,"

Always More Bang for the Buck

Even with its print ads, Whitford sought to get the most bang for its buck, devising a way to extend the shelf life of the ads. It got reprints and mailed them to its ever-growing list of customers and prospects. Again the creative approach was brief and aimed directly at customer concerns. For example, one letter attached to an ad that ran in an issue of *Housewares* read: "It takes about 90 seconds to read the attached advertisement. In that brief time, you'll discover:

1. How to cut the cost of coating cookware in half.
2. How to create a better-coated product.

It takes another 30 seconds to fill out the enclosed request for information card.

Give us two minutes of your time and we'll prove that when it comes to Xylan, time is money."

Third-Party Endorsements

While advertising allows a company to sing its praises, there is an implicit third-party endorsement in editorial content that does not attach to advertising—that is, what an objective article says about you as opposed to what you say about yourself. Most trade journals run on extremely tight budgets, often using freelance writers and photographers to keep their costs down, so there is potential for exposure on the editorial side if a company submission provides useful information, absent heavy company bias.

"So we decided to write articles of genuine technical interest to the audiences of different journals," Weir explained, "offering interesting information about how coatings—such as those made by Whitford—were solving problems in the industry in question."

Whitford has had a good deal of success getting such technical articles on topics related to specific coatings published in leading trade journals, such as *Machine Design, Product Finishing,* and *Fastener Technology.*

The articles are written as news reports and sent to editors of journals along with useful illustrative material, such as photographs, comparison charts, and the like. Often, publications use the material virtually unchanged.

"This not only gave us free publicity in the magazine, it helped establish us as the experts in a given field of problem-solving," Weir said.

Ever dedicated to extended shelf life for its marketing messages, Whitford published four-page reprints of the articles, starting with the cover of the actual magazine, followed by the two pages as published by the journal, and ending with the fourth page on why and how to contact Whitford. The company then provided the reprints to its salespeople as handouts and used them as direct mailings to show the appropriate audience what the trade journal was saying about Whitford and its products.

A Giant Step Backward

While the long-running emphasis on creating custom solutions for customers had resulted in thousands of new formulae, Xylan 1010, the coating that had launched the company, was still a major component in Whitford's arsenal. Some twenty years after its debut, however, there was concern that not only the Whitford sales force but also customers were losing touch with the product.

To regenerate interest in the coating, Weir created "The Xylan 1010 Sweepstakes," with the "1010" theme woven through it. Direct mail was used to announce it, with follow-up mailings over a period of six months. In the first letter, the prize structure was explained: "All it takes to win is your idea for a new and unusual way to use Xylan 1010—the most versatile, most dependable, most successful industrial fluoropolymer coating in the world."

First prize was $1010 worth of Xylan 1010 (about seventeen gallons). Second prize: ten ten-dollar gift certificates to McDonald's. Third prize: ten games at your favorite bowling alley (ten pins).

The first-place winner suggested, "Apply 1010 to the leading edge of small-aircraft wings to reduce ice buildup in winter and reduce disrupter air flow caused by sticking, spattered bug bodies in summer."

Once the sweepstakes ended, Whitford produced a working wristwatch on which every hour was a ten and sent it to all entrants, along with a letter thanking them and reminding them "It's always time for Xylan 1010!"

"Seven months later, we were told by one of the applicators that he had been sent a conventional wristwatch with 'DuPont Teflon' on the dial," Weir said. "We immediately saw another opportunity. We got one of the DuPont watches and photographed it next to the Xylan 1010 watch, producing a full-page illustration of the watches side by side under a headline that read, 'What time is it, anyway?' Over the Whitford watch was the caption, 'Then: August, 1991.' Over the DuPont watch was, 'Now: March, 1992.'"

This was mailed to Whitford's coaters with a letter that opened: "What time is it, anyway? We thought we agreed that it was 10:10. Now, six months later, it appears that our friends from the neighboring state (Delaware, home of DuPont's headquarters) are taking a more conventional point of view."

Solving Common Coating Problems

"As we became somewhat larger, we began to get an inferiority complex," Dave Willis said. "We began to feel we really were inferior, as our customers seemingly blamed us for all their problems. When there is a problem, most people blame it on the coating because that is where the problem shows up, since the coating is generally the last step in the manufacturing process. But ninety-nine percent of the time, it is not the coating but the way it is applied."

While Whitford's dedication to providing technical service to its customers has provided the company a competitive advantage, it comes at a cost. Troubleshooting over the phone is difficult and time consuming. Troubleshooting in person, in addition to being time consuming and difficult, is expensive. It often includes sending a technician to a customer's factory in a distant country to solve what sometimes turn out to be reasonably obvious problems.

Once again, the benefit of having an in-house agency played a significant role in an effective solution. To minimize tech-service travel expenses while not pulling back from an important customer service, Whitford created and published a forty-by-twenty-eight-inch wall chart titled Solving Common Coating Problems, which depicted the thirteen most common problems. Text under each photograph described the appearance of the problem, listed the probable causes, and suggested the solutions to solve the problem on the spot.

The company offered the poster to customers so they could review and solve their particular problems themselves, before having to ask for expensive technical help from Whitford. The posters proved so popular among Whitford's applicators in the

United States that they have been translated into many additional languages and now hang in hundreds of facilities around the world. Aside from saving potential technical-service expenses, the posters continue to reinforce Whitford as the company that knows the most about fluoropolymer coatings.

"It's so popular, it's now available in a small booklet that you can toss into your briefcase," Joan Eberhardt explained.

Sharing the Knowledge

Whitford's "Engineering Design Guide," sharing information with coating applicators worldwide.

In addition to competing head-to-head with its competitors, Whitford plays a prominent role in its industry, often producing literature that is generic to the industry and offering it to those who might benefit from it, including competitors.

Whitford's *"Engineering Design Guide,"* created years ago and updated numerous times since, is a prime example.

"For the first several years of Whitford's existence, we were effectively only in the industrial as opposed to the cookware side of the business," Willis explained. "Having come from the 'solids' side of the Teflon business, we knew quite a bit about the physical, chemical, and thermal properties of the base polymers. Almost nothing was known about the 'liquid' or coating side, as coatings were almost all used by the consumer side for food applications and were not thought of for their mechanical uses."

Within a few months of getting started, Whitford attempted to remedy this by producing a bulletin that detailed the basic properties of its first product, Xylan 1010. It included a simple series of line drawings to show the principal properties. The brochure went on to list random applications and possible substrates, including wood and paper, in addition to the more exotic metals, such as zinc and magnesium.

"As time went on," Willis said, "we were getting more useful information, mostly from our customers. That led to a decision to produce an engineering design guide. As we developed the idea and outlined the information it should contain, we realized that we only had a fraction of the 'tribal knowledge' of the industry. As the draft took shape, we mailed it to specific individuals on our industrial coaters list with a request for their comments.

We received answers and suggestions from more than thirty contributors offering personal experiences and ideas."

Over the years, the knowledge that Whitford and a variety of coaters contributed grew the guide to its current forty-four pages. It contains technical information on a wide range of subjects, including friction, release, wear, corrosion, noise reduction, substrates, application techniques, flashing, and curing, as well as calculating the real cost of a coating.

"The fact that Whitford did the work, published the booklet, and offered it free to all does a variety of things that benefit us," Weir explained. "We are the company remembered as the one ready and willing to help, and we come across as the company that knows the most about the technical aspects of the business."

Consistent Marketing on a Worldwide Basis
If the engineering design guide was a manifestation of Whitford sharing knowledge with the industry, Weir determined that sharing his knowledge internally about the whole scope of corporate communications was critical to maintaining the consistent brand identity he had worked so determinedly over so many years to achieve. Consequently, he put this wealth of knowledge down in a manual that set high standards for the company in every aspect of corporate communications.

It was entitled *The Whitford Guide to Corporate Communications*, with the subtitle *Setting the standards for communications: Who we are and why we want to keep it that way.* The fifty-seven-page manual explains in great detail what Whitford believes about communicating and why it believes it. It covers advertising content and execution, including tone of voice, layout, headlines, body copy, illustrations, and captions. It explains Whitford's approach to its logos, brochures, direct mail, typography, press releases, news articles, printing, and even letters.

"If you look at Whitford's first advertisements, done in the early 1970s, and look at what we do today, you will see a striking similarity," Weir explained. "This, too, is no accident. Because we have communicated the same kind of messages, and because we have communicated these messages in the same style, we have been able to multiply the effectiveness of our advertising."

Early photo of Tony Weir, communications director.

Whitford is now doing marketing communications in a dozen languages, a reflection of the company's growth around the world. Not surprisingly, the entity Tony Weir created at Whitford mirrors the way Whitford creates and sells its products. Rather than trying to fit the needs of the company's corporate communications into an existing "off-the-shelf" model of a client-agency relationship—not really possible given Whitford's budgets—Weir met the challenge by creating the agency within the company. In effect, a classic Whitford challenge-specific solution.

CHAPTER 14

RECRUITING AND RETAINING THE WHITFORD WAY

> *When you meet certain business leaders, you know they have that certain something.*
> —CHARLIE FIELDS, WHITFORD'S GLOBAL BUSINESS MANAGER, MEDICAL DEVICE COATINGS

How it all started for Peter Neely was decidedly different from his past job search experiences.

"During my career I had only applied for a handful of jobs," said Neely, longtime employee of Whitford UK and former managing director of the company's Asia operations, now retired. "Most interviews had been in front of as many as eight civil servants or senior managers and included psychological profiling and a second interview."

That was not the way it worked for his Whitford interview in the summer of 1995.

"I met Dave Willis and Whitford's UK general manager at a local British pub near the company's factory in Runcorn, Cheshire," Neely recalled. "The interview comprised three pints of beer, beef-and-ale pie with chips, and a general chat about me and what I could do for Whitford."

Neely's answers impressed Willis, who then asked what he was looking for in salary. Neely gave him a number.

"That's fine," Willis replied. "When can you start?"

Neely joined Whitford in England that August as worldwide quality manager.

"In hindsight," he said, "it explains a lot about Whitford and the culture that Dave has built within the company. Quick decisions, no BS, no excessive paperwork or debate—just trust, loyalty, and commitment."

A Reluctant Interviewee

While the venue may not necessarily be a British pub with "three pints of beer, beef-and-ale pie with chips," the Whitford interview experience is, as a rule, not one you'd find written up in a human resources text. Its objective, however, is always finding the right person for the job. Creating a comfort level from the outset is an important part of the experience.

When Sanjoy Pathak got an invitation to attend a Whitford job interview in December 2007, he consulted friends and colleagues at his present company. None were in favor of his attending an interview with a lesser-known company. However, sitting in his office in Kolkata, India, near the Intercontinental Hotel where the interview was scheduled, he thought, *What's the harm in checking it out?*

After a discussion of sales and marketing, Pathak was taken aside by Anne Willis, Whitford's managing director for Europe at the time and head of the company's global management team.

"I could read in her eyes that we both were ready to try each other," Pathak recalled.

Nonetheless, none of the usual factors were at play in Pathak's consideration about joining Whitford. He was already working for Linde India, a German multinational company, and he was fighting a sense of betrayal to his previous boss, who had just gotten him transferred from India's eastern region, including a promotion and a raise due shortly.

"Above all I was leaving 'almost certain' for 'uncertain,'" Pathak said. "But the most important factor, which really brought me to Whitford, was the people, and it is the people who have kept me with Whitford for years. There have been ups and downs, of course, but I am fortunate to have people who continue to keep me motivated with their words and actions. People are Whitford's main strength. Money, position, opportunity do motivate me, but not so much as the feeling of being part of this organization, where I can count my contribution in its growth and progress."

Being "Somebody" at Whitford

In addition to creating a comfort level for an interviewee whom Whitford was interested in recruiting, nurturing that into a sense of belonging started becoming part of the company's getting-acquainted dynamic from its earliest days. Chemistry at Whitford is not confined to its laboratories. To the extent that it makes people feel like they have a personal attachment to the business, it engenders a sense of loyalty that grows over the years.

When Jill Schultz began working at Whitford right out of school, the staff was small, so each member had additional job responsibilities. One of Schultz's was to pick up the mail each day at the post office, then drop off outgoing mail at the end of the day. Often the mail run would involve other errands: stop at the travel agency, go to the bank, stop at the accountants' office, and so on.

In addition, there were the chores, simply articulated aloud, for "somebody" to attend to.

"We're running low on coffee. Somebody needs to go pick up coffee, cream, sugar, and other supplies."

"Somebody needs to take this deposit to the bank."

"Can somebody drop these papers off at the travel agency or go pick up plane tickets for Dave Willis's trip?"

"Whenever I heard these statements," Schultz recalled, "I knew I was the 'somebody' going on the errands. I didn't mind, most of time, because then I was lucky enough to drive Dave Willis's car. They were always nice cars. It beat driving my '68 Buick Special or '72 Plymouth Duster."

While Schultz wasn't the only one who ran some type of errand during her early years at Whitford, those errands were a big part of her day, along with typing invoices on carbon paper, preparing lab work requests, and wrestling the old telex tape to send messages overseas.

Her stick-to-it-iveness, however, developed into the loyalty that is endemic at Whitford. Most of those early errands are accomplished today via the Internet. Such technological advancement meant many tasks that were dependent on Schultz's early errands had been eliminated. But well before that time, "somebody" had moved up the corporate ladder—her business card now reads, "Jill Schultz, Purchasing Manager."

"You Can Do It"

Sandra Quinn Kassulke first met Dave Willis in 1986, when he was looking for employees to expand Whitford's presence in Southeast Asia. Kassulke, a feisty Australian who had spent ten years with Rank Industries—a Whitford customer—was offered the job of office manager for sales in Australia and New Zealand. Despite her reservations about going from assistant to a plant manager at Rank to a management position with a different company, Willis insisted, "You can do it." She accepted.

In fact, things went so well that Willis later asked her to consider relocating to Singapore to investigate manufacturing opportunities there. Once again, Kassulke was hesitant. Coming out from behind the desk to face customers was one thing. Moving to another country to investigate manufacturing opportunities?

Once again, Willis repeated, "You can do it."

So Kassulke took on the challenge and marveled at her business card, which read "Managing Director."

"The amazing support I received from the US head office gave me the encouragement to make the move," Kassulke recalled. "My family was in awe, wasn't really sure what I was embarking on. But then again, neither was I. Dave's words, however, kept me going. I still pinch myself on just how I did what I did in Singapore. Just how did that happen? A lot of hard work, but absolutely amazing encouragement and belief in me from Dave and so many other very supportive Whitford people."

By the time Kassulke was ready to retire, Peter Neely, who was to take over as managing director, found she had assembled a great team, whose members had been brought up in the Whitford culture.

"She had done a fabulous job starting Whitford Singapore from scratch and in a short time moved to a larger factory," Neely said. "Singapore and Asia were buzzing. Everything was fast, everything was large, and our sales were growing rapidly."

Willis, however, was not ready to let her go. He interceded yet again, and Kassulke, by now an old hand at operations in the Far East, agreed to assume the role of Asia/Pacific business manager, based in Hong Kong.

A real challenge for Sandra Kassulke, as her responsibilities grew in the Far East, was dealing with Chinese customers, Asian banks, and Singaporean officials, all while she was supervising moves to new facilities.

"They had no idea how to treat a strong woman," Willis said. "She had a way to make herself known without being strident, but at the same time very clear. Sandra led the Singapore company through three moves, once every two years, negotiating with the banks and the government of Singapore for the next larger property. She made promises, and she kept them."

Women at Whitford

Dave Willis with (L-R) Joan Eberhardt, Sandra Kassulke and Anne Willis.

There are many, many examples, dating back to the company's earliest days, of Whitford assigning important positions to women.

Barbara Ficca Hayward started at Whitford in the mid-1970s as administrative assistant to cofounders Willis and Rehmeyer. By the time she retired in 1990, she had risen to treasurer and general manager.

"Dave gave women an unusual opportunity in those days," Hayward recalled. "In fact, sometimes I was the only female in a meeting, but I was present and sitting at the table. That was tremendously empowering."

The employment of women in important positions at Whitford is yet another example of a policy that emphasizes simply picking the right person for the job.

"I'm not sure we were so much ahead of our time as we were able to use the skills of the people we had," Willis said. "These women knew their jobs and grew with the responsibilities as the company grew. They saw what was needed and took the responsibilities to the larger forum. They did not let the jobs overcome them."

In those earlier years, during lean periods when the company was chronically short of cash, Ficca continually proved her mettle by keeping the funds flowing.

"Barbara would call a supplier and tell him—it was always a him—the anticipated money had not come in," Willis explained. "Then she would make a deal to delay the payment or make a partial payment with the balance to follow. Just talking to her made the other party accepting—not happy, but accepting. I do not recall us not getting what we needed when we needed it." (See chapter five.)

Consistency in Hiring, Retaining, and Promoting

When Sandra Kassulke finally did manage to retire, her valedictory comment was, "Whitford was so much more than a company. A family comes to mind, but not a family I had ever experienced."

Creating that kind of "family" chemistry, so often spoken of by Whitford employees, has been important to the company, whether hiring a top business executive domestically or abroad, production workers in the factory, or a personal assistant/secretary.

For example, Susan March came from an entry-level secretarial position and was eventually promoted to lab administrator. No easy job, but after a few weeks, she had it under control. She started with three or four people and went on to run a staff of more than twenty, always with the same level of organization, a staff with education levels ranging from high school diplomas to PhDs.

The secretarial/personal assistant position in and of itself can be vital to a company like Whitford. One of the most respected employees during the company's long history was Dolores "Dee" Jarrett, Dave Willis's personal assistant, his right hand from the mid-1960s until she retired in 2010, by then known throughout the Whitford realm as "Mother Superior."

"I first met Dave Willis in 1965, when he followed up on my 'job wanted' ad placed in a local newspaper," she said. "He was a little late. When he called, I was already two weeks into another job. It wouldn't surprise anyone who knows him that Dave's enthusiasm and persistence sold me on the idea of why I should quit that job and become part of Whitford Chemical as his 'gal Friday,' aka secretary. As I recall, with me on board, there were then a total of six employees."

In the beginning and through the early years, there were no tasks in the company that the president considered beneath him, according to Jarrett.

"He would make the coffee, wash the cups, do the dishes, empty the trash, sometimes drop off and pick up the mail," she explained. "All those normal daily activities that are required to get a new company off the ground."

When Whitford Chemical was sold to Pennwalt Corporation in 1969, Jarrett went with Pennwalt to teach its employees the ropes, but when that was completed, Willis pulled her back to the newly created Whitford Corporation.

Over the years, Jarrett was particularly impressed by the way Willis handled the development of young people.

"He would begin their journeys by opening the doors of opportunity at Whitford," she explained. "If there was a need for you at Whitford, Dave would make it happen. If there wasn't a spot, and he wanted you to join anyway, he would make a spot. Then, if there were issues you were dealing with, he would always take the time to talk them over with you. If he could lighten your load, he'd do it."

A surprise to no one at Whitford, Jarrett kept receiving job offers, some so seemingly irresistible she left Whitford on several occasions. Always, however, those who had pulled her away had no concept of Willis's tenacity when it came to Whitford people in general and Dee Jarrett in particular. Willis always found a way to get her back.

"A Hands-On Company or What?"

A president who "would make the coffee, wash the cups, do the dishes, empty the trash, sometimes drop off and pick up the mail"? Surely those sorts of daily chores for a start-up would dissipate with the growth of a successful company and the distance between buttoned-up top management and the rest of the employee corps. Well...

"A real culture shock," is how Chris Pehoviak, Whitford's managing director for Germany and manager for the consumer business in Europe, described his first days after joining the company.

"Whitford is very unorthodox in many business ways," he said. "No monthly grilling on sales, profit and loss, and costs. No ABC costing, budgets, and cost centers. No profit, profit, profit push—only a sales, sales, sales push."

While Whitford "has a different approach to managing a business," Pehoviak added, "after a while, you come to realize how practical this orientation is. Concentrate on a few simple principles, values, and practices, and the other areas of the business just fall in line."

To illustrate his introduction to Whitford, he recalls an incident at the Ambiente trade fair in Frankfurt in February 2003, a month after he started with the company. He met Dave Willis for the first time while setting up the Whitford exhibit with Anne Willis and Joan Eberhardt, from the head office in Pennsylvania.

"Just listen to Joan and Anne and do what they say, and you'll be fine," Willis had said.
Taking his own advice, Willis asked his daughter, Anne, "What can I do to help?"

"Could you clean up that deep-fat fryer so we can display it?" she answered.

"I was brand new to the company, and here was the president cleaning a deep-fat fryer!" Pehoviak said. "Is this a hands-on company or what? Dave and Anne form the culture, and it is a down-to-earth culture. Dave and the company are…the best word here is a German one: *bescheidend*." (Translations vary, Pehoviak said, between "unassuming" and "unpretentious.")

Returners in Germany

As with the best of families, sometimes the prodigal sons or daughters who have wandered off have difficulty staying away. Three women who have worked at Whitford GmbH, the company's German operation, over the years are classic examples.

Simone Wies began in the lab in 1986. With the birth of her second child in 1991, she left to spend more time with her family. By 2004, however, she was interested in a part-time position in the workforce. She began by asking if there was work available at Whitford. She was offered a position on Mondays and Tuesdays back in the lab, where she has worked ever since.

Stephanie Jung-Deisel started an apprenticeship with Whitford in August 1983. Two years later, at the end of her apprenticeship, she was employed full time.

"When you are young and working for a small company, it is very formative," she said, "since you have to deal with any number of different jobs." But by 1992, she was ready to move on and try something else. Over the years, however, she stayed in touch with Simone Wies, who had come back to Whitford.

In 2010, an orientation course for "returners" drew her back for a three-week internship at Whitford. Then in 2011, she got a call asking if she would like to return to the company. She has been working part time in customer service ever since.

After a one-year study-and-work program in the United States, Miriam Boerner started in customer service and office administration at Whitford in 1994. By the late '90s, she had developed an interest in working in marketing and took a position with another company.

With the birth of her son in 2003, Boerner began looking for part-time work that would balance well with her family commitments. She had stayed in touch with Anne Willis and former colleagues at Whitford Germany, so she inquired if they could use some marketing help. She was back with the company in April 2004.

"I liked the family atmosphere that we shared with Whitford," she said. "And although I had worked a completely different job in the past, I liked the chance to come back and work in marketing."

A Worldwide Company with No VPs?

A look at any roster of Whitford executives and department heads reveals a glaring omission. The company's executive line-up doesn't include any vice presidents. Typically Whitford, this unorthodox policy evolved as a matter of matching position and title to company needs.

"As a start-up company, we would be hiring many people that we did not know and very likely would have to move many of them into positions other than what they were hired to do," Dave Willis explained. "As we grew, some would not be up to the job we hired them for but would still have skills we could use. If they were VPs, it would be embarrassing to take away the title but keep the person."

Oddly, the policy was influenced by an unexpected development that came out of the lab.

"Our first lab director turned out to be a great chemist with almost no management skills," Willis said. "After fifty years, he is still here making contributions. We have had close to a dozen lab managers, lab directors, or other senior-sounding names, but we have never taken an officer-sounding name from someone."

Willis also had a concern about the implications of the vice president title itself.

"Being a VP generally makes someone a corporate officer with legal rights to sign for or commit the company to an action that the individual is not suited to commit to," he explained. "We have that problem in certain countries with people whose title is managing director and are officers—VPs, if you will—that sign devilish supply agreements. We have had to institute all manner of controls to keep from having trouble."

A Certain Attraction

"All through the many years we were together," said Dee Jarrett, Dave Willis's former personal assistant, "I found that no matter how trying a day Dave was having, he never took his frustrations out on me. Furthermore, in time of need, in time of trouble, he was there for all employees and their families. Whether someone needed financial assistance, had legal or medical problems or personal issues, it made no difference. Dave provided whatever support was needed. We were all part of the Whitford family, and Dave led the family. We help our own."

Jarrett always felt privileged to be at the center of things.

Dee Jarret (AKA "Mother Superior"), Dave Willis's Gal Friday for 44 years.

"I was there to keep him organized," she said, "to protect him, to try to make his day as easy as possible, as related to our department, while Dave built this great company. Dave truly appreciated the support that he received from all of us to help make Whitford the success that it is today. His generosity was always on display, not only for Whitford personnel, but their families as well. It has been my privilege and a wonderful and most rewarding experience."

Perhaps there is that certain something that resonates from a business and attracts a certain kind of employee, drawn to whatever that particular something may be: the stereotyped sharks drawn to Wall Street. Those who revel in grease-on-your-hands jobs in the great factories that built America. The computer geeks who were already fingering their parents' smart phones before they were packed off to kindergarten.

Speaking to employees at Whitford, you find those who were drawn to the company and have succeeded there were attracted by a sense that things got done at Whitford, that they could be part of the next things that got done, and that their contributions would be recognized, would be appreciated.

"You can do it," Sandra Kassulke.

You really are "somebody," Jill Schultz.

There is that sense of adventure in the "uncertain," Sanjoy Pathak.

Yes, Whitford is and always has been "hands-on," Chris Pehoviak.

We have a way to employ your marketing skills, Miriam Boerner.

And on and on.

"I am a second-generation Whitford employee," said Charlie Fields, global business manager, medical device coatings. "My father was one of the first employees."

Indeed. His father, Paul Fields, developed the Xylan 1010 formula that launched the business. (See chapter three.)

"I have known the Willis family my entire life," Fields continued. "I have been in the fluoropolymer/high performance coatings/plastics industry for thirty years—twenty in operations and ten years in sales and market development. In 2012, I had the chance to join Whitford, a lifelong goal."

Fields said he had always wanted to work for Dave Willis. "I told him that many times, and I finally got the opportunity. A lot of people share that attitude, and I think that is Dave's biggest legacy. He has had a serious impact on everything in my career. When you meet certain business leaders, you know they have that certain something."

CHAPTER 15

A Long-Established Global Presence

Change comes about with globalization and the recognition that we have to have uniform products across the globe.
—MICHAEL COATES, WHITFORD'S WORLDWIDE BUSINESS DEVELOPMENT MANAGER

The executive conference room at Whitford Worldwide's Elverson, Pennsylvania, headquarters features a map with all the company locations identified by flags. While Whitford is not a giant multinational, it definitely has an impressive global presence. To a significant degree, Whitford's global representation is a result of a cofounder's wanderlust, established very early on.

"I probably owe this to my parents," Dave Willis explained. "Both had traveled to Europe when they were young, my mother in a first-class cabin, my father jumping ship in Rotterdam and spending the summer roaming the Continent."

Willis's parents were concerned that their two sons, as Americans, would not know anything about the rest of the world. So they decided to take Dave and his brother on a European trip.

"Since then," Willis said, "my best guess is that I have been to Europe more than two hundred times, Hong Kong one hundred times, Brazil thirty. My parents succeeded beyond their wildest dreams."

While Willis's wanderlust may have begun as a personal interest, projecting his company's expansion abroad was simply good business. Whitford moved toward global sales because its markets were expanding globally. As Whitford's litany of formulae increased, worldwide demand for its products followed suit.

"We were always looking for new business," he said. "When the Boeing 707 had taken over the air lanes in 1958 through '60, it had become easy to get almost any place and to do so quickly. And the fares were not too crazy."

So Willis began a decades-long travel schedule, during which he accumulated more than 5 million miles in the air, more than 3.5 million on United Airlines alone.

Risk versus Reward Overseas

Whitford Corporation had started in the last two months of 1969 and by 1970 already had overseas inquiries, generating a sales trip by Willis to the United Kingdom that spring. He was convinced early on that it was time to establish an international presence. When you have a new company with extremely limited resources, your options tend to be limited. However, sometimes luck plays a role, and a solution is close at hand. In Whitford's case, a convergence of career interests played a key role.

When John Powell, a classmate of Whitford's cofounder Ted Rehmeyer in the MBA program at the University of Pennsylvania, approached the partners about considering him to set up a Whitford operation in the United Kingdom, they agreed, and Whitford Plastics, Ltd. was born in 1970. That business continued to grow at an industrial site in Runcorn, Cheshire. (See chapter two.)

When General Electric relocated some of its small-appliance operations to Brazil, Whitford set up an operation there in 1986. By the mid-1980s, companies began to shut down in the United States and move operations to Asia, and Whitford followed there as well, establishing a presence in Singapore.

"We took some risks going into Brazil and Singapore," Willis said, "but the risks were less than they appeared, as we had already been in those markets for ten years in a limited way. We had some great support from our suppliers. Extended credit terms were an enormous help. Banks and banking relationships contributed—albeit unevenly—to our ability to grow. We concentrated on the business we were in and did not try to expand into businesses that looked good but where we had nothing special to bring to the party. We hired some really good people over the years, and we worked very hard at customer service."

"Originally, we set up in Singapore not so much as a manufacturing operation but as a warehousing facility, and then it just grew rapidly," said Larry Leech, who held multiple positions at Whitford across a career of more than forty years.

"Singapore was really the right place for Whitford to begin operations in Asia," he explained, "because it was the only way to get Americans over there to work and live. It was clean and attractive and had a good work environment. And everyone spoke English. I am sure it was not the most economical place to set up business at that time, but our business grew so rapidly that even if it cost us more to do it, we had a place to do it in. That proved to be a godsend."

A Major Acquisition

While spotting footholds in key locations around the world, then slowly growing those offices to meet demand, Whitford also took on mergers, acquisitions, and joint ventures where they meant market penetration for its product line. The company's merger in 1998 with Becherplast in Italy, for example, created greater outlets for its products in Europe, the Middle East, and Africa. (See chapter ten.) Then in 2009, Whitford completed its largest acquisition.

AkzoNobel is the largest paint company in the world. A tiny portion of its business was in nonstick coatings, and that began to look like an attractive acquisition target in support of Whitford's global expansion, especially in terms of the company's business in cookware coatings. Whitford began negotiating to buy that piece of business in the second quarter of 2008 and closed the deal in September of 2009. The acquisition was by far Whitford's largest, increasing its sales volume by close to $40 million.

"Although it is a solid business, our nonstick coatings operation does not have the scale for it to become a true market leader globally," explained Leif Darner, the AkzoNobel board member responsible for performance coatings. "In the hands of new owners, however, it offers good growth opportunities, and we are convinced our employees are joining an ambitious and successful company run by capable professionals who we trust to take the business forward."

The acquisition included sites in the United States, Italy, China, Brazil, and India, in essence extending Whitford's reach around the world. A significant amount of the Akzo business was at its manufacturing site in Fombio, Italy, which would involve consolidating production with Whitford's existing Italian operation. In order to manage the additional growth, Whitford Italy built a warehouse and research and development labs and added areas for manufacturing and office space. The company also hired some of Akzo's key coating personnel.

Integrating Akzo into Whitford's Italian operation became a huge challenge for Chicco Vallaperta, head of Whitford Italy.

"We had employees who worked for us for twenty-five or thirty years," he said. "Certainly they had to adjust. Then there were the new people we needed to make feel comfortable in their new location. And most important of all, we had to pursue business success as a team. So the integration of the two groups was important."

Within four years, the Akzo operation was fully integrated into Whitford Italy, and sales had doubled. Today, it supplies the lion's share of the company's cookware coatings sold in Europe. In the process, Whitford Italy has grown to become Whitford's fourth largest facility in terms of sales.

"Finally, we had the presence in this key European market that we had wanted for many years," Dave Willis said.

An Important Joint Venture

In 2006, Whitford entered into a joint venture with Advanced Flexible Composites, based in Lake in the Hills, Illinois, with the joint venture aspect of the arrangement housed in Whitford's Runcorn, England, facility. Called Whitford Flexible Composites (WFC), the venture is a technology transfer and supply agreement. The formation of WFC further solidified a long partnership Whitford has had with AFC and extended Whitford's already extensive product line yet again on an international stage.

A family-owned-and-operated company, AFC was founded in 1988 and became a world leader in the manufacture of high-performance coated and laminated fabrics. The company designs and manufactures PTFE- and silicone-coated fabrics and belting, along with an extensive line of pressure-sensitive tapes for use in diverse applications. Typical applications for its products are found in industries such as aerospace, flexible packaging, screen printing, textiles, polymer manufacturing, food processing, chemical, electronics, and communications.

"AFC is extremely pleased with the opportunity to partner with what we believe to be the world leader in the development of high-performance, nonstick coatings," AFC's CEO William Lewis said at the time of the alliance. "Whitford's international expertise and unrivaled ability to conceive and formulate high-performance nonstick coatings, combined with AFC's well-known ability to deliver innovative, high-quality products with the shortest of lead times, creates a powerful company capable of developing innovative products to meet the demanding needs of customers."

WFC coatings are principally formulated for the belting market, specializing in food-industry applications. The company's sheets and belts regularly handle the high temperatures and rigors of the food-processing environment, facilitating the flow of materials while providing excellent release properties and resistance to chemicals and oils. Working with WFC, Whitford has developed several proprietary coatings that offer better release and increased resistance to penetration by hot oil and grease.

Meanwhile an exciting new opportunity has arisen with the growing importance of wind-powered energy. Because of its unmatched release characteristics, WFC coated glass is being used to line the molds for the blades of the world's largest offshore wind turbine manufacturer. (See chapter nine.)

Expanding into Canada

In January 2011, Whitford gained a significant presence in Canada completing its purchase of the outstanding shares of HP Polymers, a leading manufacturer of a variety of resins. Located in Guelph, Ontario, HP manufactures specialty high-temperature polymers used by coating manufacturers around the world for a wide variety of applications.

The purchase added significant versatility to Whitford's product line. HP's varnishes and specialty resins are used for coatings on a wide assortment of products, from paper to concrete, plastic to metal, and wood finishes for everything from kitchen cabinets to high-end furniture.

Its ink resins are compounded for lithographic printing applications, designed to provide high gloss, rapid setting, and excellent printability. They are used in the manufacture of sheet-fed, web heat-set, plastic, moisture-set, and rubber-based inks. The inks are used on a wide range of packaging products. Other resins are used in high-quality lithographic inks for posters, magazines, and brochures.

Products are made to order in quantities from small batches to truckloads, with short delivery cycles—two weeks or less—to facilitate the path from initial concept to design, then production.

International before It Became Fashionable
Whitford's committed international vision has been an important element in the company's success from the very beginning, according to Chris Annas, Whitford's first banker at Industrial Valley Bank in West Chester, Pennsylvania.

"The international thrust of Whitford during its early years has really paid off," said Annas, now CEO of Meridian Bank. "The company has gotten bigger because it has been established around the world for years, and it has worked to develop new customers in all of its markets as they have evolved. Whitford was international before it became fashionable. The company found markets in many countries through heavy travel schedules and then putting boots on the ground."

In charge of "boots on the ground" in Europe for more than two decades has been Anne Willis, and that has included continuing to expand the company's market penetration, even when the landscape becomes forbidding, as it did during the economic downturn that began in 2008.

Dave & Anne Willis, Russia, 2008.

"We spent a couple of years upgrading our facilities and taking advantage of quality people being out of jobs," she explained. "We have spent a good deal on training and getting people—sales, customer service, production, technical, IT, et cetera—at all stages of the process to be prepared for business to increase. The increase in business started the first part of 2014 in the UK, and we continue to produce record weeks and months."

By continually following a mantra of not standing down, the company is consistently in a position to take advantage of opportunities that others, who have pulled back, cannot address.

"Prior to the formation of the EU, many companies shifted manufacturing to China to gain the benefits from cheaper production," Anne Willis said. "Then, with cash being tight and lean manufacturing being used by all, this backfired, as lead times became too long, and Chinese wages increased. The companies that began bringing their manufacturing back were ending up in central Europe—non-EU-regulated countries—where it is the best of both worlds: on the doorstep, at the right price, without the costly regulations. This has helped us regain a degree of control."

Fighting the "Silo Mentality"

With the expansion of Whitford's overseas presence and a growing list of customers on a global scale, maintaining a coordinated effort that recognizes cultural, political, and economic diversities, while also trying to maintain a consistent brand image, can be challenging, to say the least. Whitford products are created in labs on different continents and produced in its facilities across the globe. Whitford's markets are both near and far, comprising many, many individual customers all over the world. Facilities scattered around the world may tend to develop a "silo mentality"—each location standing alone and not willing to collaborate. Fostering teamwork is an ongoing challenge within such a mentality, which could have dire consequences for the business as a whole.

"We have more than thirteen hundred product lines, which include nine thousand individual products among them, marketed under fifty brand names," said Michael Coates, Whitford's worldwide business development manager. "Change comes about with globalization and the recognition that we have to have uniform products across the globe. Maintaining a coordinated effort is essential to our success."

Coates said maintaining that coordination becomes a matter of continuous electronic communication, including the use of international teleconferencing among Whitford locations, which occurs on virtually a daily basis. However, maintaining personal contact is also critical to sharing important information, and Whitford has always been a company that travels, even during economic downturns when its competitors cut back.

Work Hard/Play Hard

"Work hard/play hard" has oftentimes been used to justify over-the-top behavior by successful groups in high-paying, high-pressure jobs or even students of the wealthy at elite private schools or universities when away from their work-hard settings. *The Urban Dictionary* describes such behavior as providing "an excuse for mindless partying directing one's life without any space for taking anything seriously in the world."

Not all time at Whitford is spent working hard.

Like so much of how Whitford deals with its world, the company turns this definition on its head. At Whitford, taking the world seriously is what has led the company, from its most senior executives on down, to make "play hard" bind the corporate family together. Playing hard to reinforce these ties that bind is particularly effective in bringing together employees from the far-flung corners of the corporate realm and intensifying their sense of family.

Formulating and testing coatings, for example, is difficult, detailed, and sometimes tedious work. So every few years, a worldwide technical meeting is held, at which members of all the company's laboratories meet and talk about new products, problems, solutions, and any other issues they might be having. At the same time, senior management at Whitford will waste no opportunity to reinforce the company's sense of corporate family.

"To make these trips more memorable and to force the scientific types out of their comfort zone, a themed, and often costumed, dinner is held," reported Dr. Leonard Harvey, worldwide technical manager, having himself been the pope among a gathering of gods in togas at one such meeting in Brescia, Italy.

Managers' meetings in such far-flung places as Capetown, South Africa; St. Petersburg, Russia; Cartagena, Colombia; Prague, Czech Republic and even on a cruise in the Adriatic have helped cement this sense of belonging.

"We hold these meetings in various places around the world for a number of reasons," Anne Willis explained. "One is to get to know each other better personally. And that means we can't be in meetings all day."

Tax on Foreign Profits

Of course, doing business around the world, while a necessity for a company like Whitford, also creates complex regulation and tax issues. An ongoing favorite among the topics for political bluster in the United States is railing against companies shifting American jobs overseas. Those opposed to this "inversion" argue it is simply an effort by corporations to maximize profits by replacing well-paid American workers with much cheaper labor abroad. They press for heavy taxes on corporations that do this.

However, the drug giant Pfizer, trying to make the case to allow its mega merger with Dublin-based Allergan and relocate its headquarters to Ireland, argued that while the move would significantly cut its tax bill, it also would allow the company to invest more in the United States, ultimately adding jobs domestically. The Pfizer-Allergan merger ultimately failed, but Whitford provides an example of the validity of the argument Pfizer used.

Whitford is much smaller than the two giant drug companies and not publicly traded. Nonetheless, the company does business in forty countries, shipping from manufacturing facilities in the United States, Canada, the United Kingdom, Italy, Brazil, China, India, and Singapore. It has additional sales offices in France, Germany, Spain, Turkey, Colombia, Hong Kong, Vietnam, Mexico, and China.

"We followed our customers as they went overseas," Dave Willis said. "We now do about seventy-five percent of our business outside of the US. Our locations in these many countries are used to serve our customers who are located there. Many of those customers are subsidiaries of US companies; others are locally owned and operated organizations. Our customers demand delivery within ten days of our receipt of their order. Because we have local production throughout the world, we are able to meet that need."

Whitford's products are relatively heavy, and many are considered hazardous, so airfreight would not be an option, even if it were not prohibitively expensive. Shipping product manufactured in the United States by sea to foreign-based customers also is not a viable option when competing with large, well-financed competitors headquartered in Germany and Switzerland and many, much-smaller local competitors around the world, that can and do provide very quick delivery. A sea journey would take between six and eight weeks, depending on where the customers were located. That time in transit would be unacceptable for much of the business overseas. That in turn would affect Whitford's employment levels in the United States.

"There is no way we could be the size we are, employing about two hundred people in the US, without the foreign facilities," Willis said. "Many of our US employees are technical research and development people who formulate coatings for the US, as well as the overseas locations. We have maintained our US R&D facility at substantial cost over moving it to the UK or Singapore, despite the fact that both locations have the available technical skills and most of the production and analytical equipment to do what the US does."

Whitford's initial overseas expansion method was to invest a small amount of permanent capital and allow the new foreign locations to buy raw materials from the United States, then repay what in effect was a loan as they were able to do so. For example, at one point, Whitford Singapore "owed" Whitford US more than $1 million. This effectively supplied sufficient working capital for the Singapore operation to exist until income and profits allowed for borrowing locally to repay the United States. Future growth then came from locally generated profits.

As the initial foreign operations became profitable, they were able to fund sales offices where needed. Because these funds had been treated as loans as opposed to capital, they were repaid without taxes from the foreign location. This same technique was used to fund entry and growth in China. The ability to "leave" the money in the various companies around the world was the way growth was accomplished.

"As the current law is written," Willis explained, "if we want to, or need to, spend the profits we've earned overseas in the US, we are required to pay the difference between the tax rate paid and the US tax rate of forty percent on all income repatriated. Should the current law change to preclude our ability to leave profits in our foreign affiliates, we do not believe we will have enough money to run our business, let alone expand in the normal course of business. While at the same time our German and Swiss competitors have significantly more funds to use to grow or repatriate without tax to their home country. The local companies pay local taxes and move ahead."

Fashionably Successful
Whether the company is measuring risks versus rewards, following customers as they relocate, adding new foreign customers, building facilities abroad and recruiting the best people to staff operations near and far, or dealing with a dizzying array of regulations and tax laws, functioning globally is nothing less than a necessity for Whitford Worldwide.

If Whitford was international before it became fashionable, as banker Chris Annas put it, then international has been very good to Whitford. The company's success at expanding overseas is a virtual how-to for dealing with globalization. So perhaps "fashionable" can be viewed as a synonym for "successful," and Dave Willis's parents' concern about their son not knowing anything about the rest of the world has long since been put to rest many times over.

CHAPTER 16

THE CUSTOMER IS ALWAYS...

> *There is only one boss. The customer. And he can fire everybody in the company from the chairman on down, simply by spending his money somewhere else.*
> —SAM WALTON

Don Peppers and Martha Rogers, who have made a career out of writing about "customer centricity," are quoted as having said, "Some customers are more equal than others."[9] Assessing a customer's impact on a company's profitability, including the projected long-term value of the company's relationship with a customer, has been the subject of MBA classes, countless analyses, essays, business books, computer models, and on and on.

The Wharton School at the University of Pennsylvania even offers a workshop in customer lifetime value that explains:

> "CLV is a critical concept for virtually every organization that claims (or aspires) to be customer centric. At a granular

---

9 "Customer Centricity versus Customer Experience." Don Peppers and Martha Rogers, Peppers & Rogers Group, September 28, 2012, http://www.peppersandrogersgroup.com/view.aspx?DocID=33880.

level, it helps companies decide which tactics should be used for which customer; at a more macro level, it is the key ingredient in calculating customer equity—which, in turn, drives overall corporate valuation…Our coverage of probability models will be woven into the workshop as a 'means toward an end' with modest (and 'manager friendly') handling of the technical details and model implementation in Excel."

When discussing customer relationships at Whitford, one would be very unlikely to hear terms like "customer centricity," "granular level," or "probability models." If there is a single, overriding philosophy apparent in how Whitford approaches customer relationships, it is a collaborative effort to find the best solutions to specific customer needs, immediate, near term, and long term.

"I get excited about my customers' projects just as much as they do," said Suzie Eberhardt of Whitford's retail marketing team. "It helps when our team is involved early in the development process. The earlier we can get involved, the better. We have a great team at Whitford that has most of the answers. If I don't have the answer, there is definitely someone here who does."

In effect, call this Whitford's variation on the CLV theme. The result, beginning long before computer probability models and flourishing at Whitford for decades, has been legions of diehard customers.

CLV at Whitford

It was 1970, and Whitford Corporation had barely opened its doors when Dave Willis showed up at the factory of Crest Coatings, a DuPont-approved applicator in southern California. Crest itself was barely three years old.

"Dave had a quart of Xylan 1010," said Mike Erickson, Crest CEO. "He said, 'Here, try this.' We tried it on a couple of jobs, and it worked well. That created a dialogue with him. Back then, he was doing all the sales, so we'd see him every six months or so, out on the West Coast. He'd share with us any new developments that he had."

As Crest started using Xylan 1010, the company began looking at other products that Whitford had as well. Then the process evolved into Whitford working with Crest to develop products for specific needs. But...

"The engineer at a customer that made crepe pans had miscalculated the temperature on the surface by some two hundred degrees Fahrenheit," Erickson explained, "so the material that Dave had originally thought would do the job started turning white and chalking, which didn't make the customer very happy. So Whitford hustled out a new product made specifically for that application. Dave knew what his product was and what we were trying to accomplish. With the shipment of the first couple of gallons, Dave and one of his engineers flew out and spent a couple of days with us to figure out how to make this new material work. They knew it would have the temperature resistance but were not real sure what the pretreatment would be. We figured that all out. It wasn't very long after when we got this data sheet, and there's this new material in the Whitford catalog with all the stuff we had worked on."

Erickson was very impressed with this level of attention, something he just couldn't get from the big companies in the industry.

"DuPont had such a cumbersome path you had to go through to get something like that done," he said. "First, you had to get with the sales guy. You had to give him the projected numbers, and they had to be big enough that DuPont deemed it was worth their while. Then there were minimum charges and minimum gallon orders. If you wanted a color match of an existing material, you had to order thirty gallons, which was a big number. Whitford would mix you up one gallon of a special color. Whitford was very different from the other alternatives when it came to coming up with a new material that met a need. We got to the point where we didn't even call anyone else when we had any kind of special application. The whole job would go away before the big boys would even get started on the program."

Staying Connected

Bruce Nesbitt is chairman of Chicago-based Orion Industries, a registered, approved applicator of Xylan and more than five hundred other functional coatings. Orion has been a Whitford customer for many years.

Long-time customer, Bruce Nesbitt, chairman Orion Industries.

"It's fairly remarkable to call a company, after decades and decades, to find the very same voice on the other end of the phone," Nesbitt said. "When other companies, such as DuPont, cut back on their sales staff, Whitford took the opposite approach, going after a market that was rapidly developing. It required close and personal relationships with engineers, designers, and customers that use functional coatings."

Then there is the level of personal attention Whitford devotes to its customers.

"I remember in the '70s and '80s when the Whitford sales staff would come by every three to four weeks and would immediately see you about new projects," he said. "This certainly cemented the bond between us and their field salesmen, as well as the technical staff and order processors at Whitford headquarters. Everybody was on a first-name basis."

Nesbitt added that he also has been impressed with Whitford's intense level of customer support and problem-solving procedures.

"The Whitford staff is able to categorize problems and provide great assistance about not only what to do but what not to do with a prospective coating," he said. "The other competitors have a small line of good coatings that are listed on a product-offering sheet. Whitford has a mind-boggling number of products that would take a CIA analyst to stay on top of. That's what differentiates them."

Nesbitt is convinced, however, that the product line would be just that confusing were it not for the field salespeople who help turn the theoretical into problem solutions.

"They have field sales staff, to which we have access, who are knowledgeable about products that we might never talk about in the normal course of business," he explained. "For example, take automotive fasteners. Their research people have developed coatings for auto fasteners that are really on the cutting edge of corrosion resistance. Their sales staff can quickly and clearly respond to the technical questions our people might have. The competitors take days to get back to you, and they only seem to know just about as much as you can find on a data sheet—and no more."

Building a History Together
"If there is a choice between using a Whitford material and using DuPont or another supplier, we will choose Whitford," said Tim Kissling, president of Precision Coating Technology and Manufacturing (PCTM). "Usually, price has little to do with the choice. Quality, service, and delivery are the key reasons."

Kissling and Whitford have a long history together. They grew into their respective businesses not far from each other in Pennsylvania, on parallel tracks that go back to the earliest days of Whitford Corporation and Kissling's entry into the coating-applications industry, first as an employee, then as a business owner.

"Beginning in 1974, I worked for fourteen years as sales manager for Fusion Coatings, a powder-coating company," Kissling said. "During this time, I was introduced to Ron Seitzinger, sales manager for Whitford, who was good friends with Fusion's owner, Ken Harms. Ron and I collaborated on a number of projects that involved both of our companies. In 1986, Ken Harms retired and sold Fusion Coatings. Two years later, I left and started PCTM."

As part of Harms's agreement with the new owner, he could not collaborate with former employees of Fusion Coatings. So Kissling sought out trusted individuals to use as an "informal board of directors" to help get his new company started. He chose Seitzinger as one of them.

"For years PCTM was a small company—less than ten employees—and was struggling to survive," Kissling said. "As such, we took whatever jobs came our way. For the most part, that meant using more common finishing materials, i.e., traditional powder coatings as opposed to the 'engineered finishes' that Whitford produced. Nevertheless, we maintained a working relationship with Whitford with the idea that in the long term, it would be beneficial to include Whitford's engineered finishes as part of PCTM's offerings to the marketplace."

By 2009, things had turned around for PCTM to the point at which the company could purchase a forty-eight-thousand-square-foot facility in Denver, Pennsylvania.

"In so doing," Kissling explained, "we were able to expand our capabilities to add a wider spectrum of finishes that included most of the Whitford product line. Today, PCTM is a $3.5 million business employing thirty people, and thirty percent of our business is dedicated to applying high-performance engineered finishes, such as those offered by Whitford."

Close Customer Contact

Whitford's relationship with its customers is very much a matter of working together as a team.

"There are a number of different ways to get information from a company you do business with," said Mario DiSalvo, product-development manager for All-Clad Metalcrafters. "The opportunity to go to that company—to speak with the staff, to get to know the people that are working day to day at the facility, to discuss not only your application but also future opportunities—is just a big benefit."

All-Clad is a high-end home goods manufacturer based in Canonsburg, Pennsylvania. The company markets its products, including cookware, ovenware, kitchen tools, and accessories, around the world.

"Whitford is a practice-what-they-preach organization," DiSalvo said. "They are very process oriented. As you would expect, it is an extremely clean environment. The people I have worked with are well organized, professional, and generous with all kinds of information. In fact, they are collaborative; they work with you to find the best solution, and they stay in touch to make sure that the solution continues to work."

The Value of an Educated Customer

Sandra Daigle is technical sales account manager at Sun Belt Coatings, a job shop in Cleveland, Tennessee. After more than fifteen years of dealing with Whitford over the phone or through visiting company representatives, she attended one of the programs at Whitford University, the classroom and lab sessions the company conducts for customers. (See chapter twelve.)

"Having transitioned out of a quality role—I was a quality manager for seven years—and moving into the sales department, I went to the Whitford University sessions with the intention of getting more familiar with the industrial coatings and applications that we sell, so I could better inform our customers about what coatings are best for their products," she explained. "The entire session was extremely well done. I know that a large percentage of Whitford's business is in cookware coatings, and even though we don't sell those coatings, it was interesting and valuable to learn how they are used. In fact, there really is some crossover with their finishes, so some industrial finishes are used in consumer applications and vice versa."

One of the best things about the training, according to Daigle, was that it interwove a lecture component with an activity component.

"They opened up their whole facility and broke the session into small groups," she said. "Each group circulated, so we all had an experience with various parts of their operations. In some cases, they actually put a spray gun or a powder gun in our hands and let us coat a part. We talked to researchers. We talked to product managers. We talked to people in charge of various aspects of coating development and coating production. It felt like we saw everything that goes on, from the development of a new product to full production to how they continue to support that product with their customers."

One of the other elements that impressed Daigle was that Whitford had many of its own new employees go through the same training.

"As a customer and an applicator, I was surrounded not only by my peers in the industry but also by Whitford employees," she said. "This diversity of various backgrounds enhances the entire experience. And it also shows how Whitford invests in its employees."

Customer-Driven Emphasis

Marcel Klutke is president of Reinhold Industries Ltd. of Edmonton, Alberta, Canada. The company has more than thirty years of experience in servicing the oil and gas industries in both Canada and the United States. It is a leader in custom machining and produces its own product line of tubular goods and wellhead flow-control equipment. Klutke said that Whitford's coatings help his company give his customers longer service life with their equipment. Klutke also attended a Whitford University session.

"One of the strongest impressions I took away is how customer-driven Whitford is," he said. "These sessions clearly illustrate what their products can do for me and my customers. That's a value that goes straight to the bottom line. I was amazed at all the product applications and businesses that use Whitford coatings. The equipment in their facility is state of the art. Take color, for example. Some of their customers are incredibly particular about a color, and that requires very precise measuring, mixing, and inspections that are altogether just mind boggling."

Educating customers about Whitford's products, as well as providing the wherewithal for them to interact with Whitford employees in classroom and lab settings, may reflect what Mike Miller, former COO and the major mover behind Whitford University, called "enlightened self-interest," but it is another manifestation of the company staying close to its customers.

From the earliest days of Whitford's existence, as new customers become acquainted with its coatings, Whitford's sales efforts have included joint calls with applicators, providing them the added benefit of taking a coating expert with them as they sought new business. Further, it is not uncommon for Whitford customers—particularly in the oil and gas and auto industries—to ask for Whitford's help in writing their specs for coatings. As a result, as customers turn into repeat users of Whitford's products, there is an ongoing appreciation for the personal attention they receive on so many fronts.

Dealing with Complaints, Quickly and Effectively

Sir Colin Marshall, whose long career in business included senior positions at a number of global companies, including CEO of British Airways, certainly had his share of stressful situations. His conclusion? "The customer doesn't expect everything will go right all the time; the big test is what you do when things go wrong." Anyone who has been in business for a considerable length of time understands that dealing with adversity is the acid test in customer relationships. How you deal with complaints is critical to a long-term positive relationship with customers.

At Whitford facilities, a chart can be found on the walls entitled "How to react to customer complaints." It lays out six points: Defuse the situation. Define the problem. Document the problem. Communicate the problem. Solve the problem. Follow up.

"When customers have some coating in their shop that they can't use, it puts them behind, and they have a tendency to get desperate," explained Herb Ferguson, Whitford's inside technical sales representative. "We are slowing them down, and they are not able to make money. So one of the things that we do here is to quickly get in touch with the customer and understand his or her needs for resolving the issue in a timely fashion."

Perhaps the key element in doing that is to duplicate the malfunction. The quality-control department at Whitford retains samples of every batch of coating that goes out the door for a minimum of one year. When a complaint is registered, QC examines the relevant coating sample. Often the problem is a result of the misapplication of the coating, and testing the samples can help determine how the customer can resolve the issue.

For example, when a cookware customer complained that the color of the coating was too dark, Whitford QC sprayed the relevant sample on test panels, then cured the panels for different time periods. The tests revealed the customer was not curing the cookware long enough.

"We advised the customer to slow down the conveyor line speed," Ferguson explained. "There are 'fugitives' in the coating that have to be burned out. If they are not, you have color variations. That solved the problem. Sometimes when you are trying to get so many pans out in a day, one way to do that is to speed up your line. However there can be unwanted consequences."

Customer Complaints: An Upside?

On the other hand, there can be an upside to negative experiences. Bill Gates, whose Microsoft has had to deal with its share of customer complaints over the years, has said, "Your most unhappy customers are your greatest source of learning." Whitford has a similar outlook about lessons learned.

"If the customer's complaint is substantiated, we confirm the batch was not any good, then we make arrangements to credit the customer's account and try to expedite material to them," Ferguson said. In the aftermath of such substantiated issues, he cited cases where customer complaints have resulted in Whitford improving procedures on batch labeling, equipment cleanliness, and packaging procedures, among others.

Improving procedures to minimize faulty product has an impact on cost controls, according to Amy Reilly, Whitford's senior customer service representative. "If we have to pay to dispose of the material, we have to send a truck, and that costs a lot of money," she said. "We have a complaint task force that meets once a week to make sure that every complaint is gone over and communicated back to the customer, verifying that things are not falling by the wayside."

Once They're Gone...
When substantiated problems do occur, the importance not only of remedying the immediate problem for the customer but also of using the issue as a learning experience to prevent similar issues in the future cannot be overstated. Once a customer has developed a decidedly negative opinion of your output, convincing the customer otherwise can be a long, expensive, and energy-consuming process.

Whitford's loss of the Meyer Manufacturing business in 1978 was a blow that took down 40 percent of its sales and nearly devastated the company. (See chapter five.) The fact that the problem with the coating Whitford sold to Meyer was the result of a resin altered by Phillips Petroleum, a Whitford supplier, did not mitigate the situation with Meyer. What mattered to the customer was that the coating no longer worked on its cookware. While Whitford managed to succeed in a legal action against Phillips and instituted strict safeguards for incoming raw materials, the Meyer business had already been lost. After righting its faltering ship, Whitford went back to work to convince Meyer it deserved another chance. Although the giant Asian company eventually returned to the fold, it took twenty-three years.

Providing Some General Assistance

While it is not unusual for companies to listen to their customers' problems, complaints, or other issues, what is unusual is how far Whitford goes above and beyond for its customers. For example, Whitford's US customers have to file information with their home states each year on the emissions of volatile organic compounds (VOCs) into the atmosphere. It's a complicated and highly technical task, but it must be done. Whitford has all that data as part of the company's production records.

"We compile the data to suit their needs," Dave Willis explained. "We supply that information to them in the exact form that they need to fill out their documents. We do the work for them. All we do is change the format of our data to fit their needs."

Whitford sends a letter each year pointing out that the company can supply this information in whatever manner the customer needs: paper, electronic, or disc.

"That idea came from a customer," Willis said, "but for some reason, our competitors still don't do it. Simple and easy for Whitford to do, but enormously helpful to our customers. The idea, in other words, came from listening. And the practice of the idea comes from the focus on solving problems for customers."

Evolution, Sort of...

Interaction between Whitford and its customers is an ongoing learning experience, even after more than a half century of relationships with many, many customers. While there is a powerful evolving element to how a successful company treats customers, in Whitford's case there is a core principal that has played a significant role in defining the relationship from the very beginning. It is a matter of making it clear that Whitford really cares about its customers' success and will partner with them to achieve that. That partnership spans the breadth of the relationship, beginning with the initial sale, on to the process of defining products to address specific needs, to altering products and processes that do not work, then beginning the whole process over again with new products or introducing Whitford to new customers.

"Whitford sales staff would come by every three to four weeks and would immediately see you about new projects."—Bruce Nesbitt, chairman of Orion Industries

"They are collaborative; they work with you to find the best solution, and they stay in touch to make sure that the solution continues to work."—Mario DiSalvo, product-development manager for All-Clad Metalcrafters

"One of the strongest impressions I took away is how customer driven Whitford is."—Marcel Klutke, president of Reinhold Industries Ltd.

"Usually, price has little to do with the choice. Quality, service, and delivery are the key reasons."—Tim Kissling, Precision Coating Technology and Manufacturing

If "customer-centric selling" is having meaningful, one-on-one relationships with customers and then following up with a high level of support after the sale, Whitford has been doing that since long before such a modus operandi had an academic term attached to it. In the process, Whitford has had an outsize influence on the coatings industry in general.

"Dave Willis really expanded the use of fluoropolymer coatings by allowing us to identify a need and then coming up with a material that was nonexistent at the time," said Mike Erickson of Crest Coatings. "If it hadn't been for Whitford, I really think the scope of fluoropolymer coatings would be a lot less than it is today."

CHAPTER 17

Xylan's Extended Family

A kinship group consisting of a family nucleus and various relatives... and functioning as a larger unit.
—Dictionary.com

Big-picture perspective comes with the hindsight of fifty-plus years. If "never forget where you came from" is advice with both supporters and detractors, it nonetheless provides for significant historical context at Whitford. While the creation of Xylan 1010 established the viability of the company that would become Whitford Worldwide, the expansion of the Xylan family over the years reads like a plot synopsis of the greater Whitford story. Xylan 1010 was the first matrix coating based on engineered polymers. The genius of the product was its ability to create a usable platform for polytetrafluoroethylene (PTFE), a polymer that, in and of itself, was not very useful. But if the story began there, it was a beginning that held on to its relevance. Xylan has managed to ensure that Whitford never forgets where the company came from. Over the ensuing years, Xylan 1010 has sired an extended family of thousands of coatings, matrix structures that combine tough, high-temperature engineered polymers with long-chain dry lubricants.

"We have about twenty-five hundred active formulas for Xylan in the US alone," said Brian Willis, who is in charge of inside sales at Whitford. "We tend to introduce about three hundred a year and make about three hundred inactive per year, but we can always reactivate a formula if required."

That Xylan 1010 would be anything more than a single product was not contemplated at the time of its creation.

"I don't think we thought about it," Dave Willis recalled. "We had a coating system, even if we did not know it at the time. Essentially, we took the system and made it work for us."

What they had was something truly revolutionary. What they'd accomplished was taking a chemical with great potential but no effective avenue to pursue that potential and creating its forward motion. While tests documented that PTFE had a very low coefficient of friction, early on there were challenges to creating PTFE coatings that could be useful in industrial applications. An early Whitford report stated the problems: "The polymer is soft and tends to cold flow under modest loads. Because the material is soft, it is rapidly worn away."

But that all changed in 1969. The report went on: "A new type of coating—really a matrix structure—was developed that had five to seven times the wear resistance of the earlier finishes. Called Xylan, the result is a composite with the friction characteristics of fluorocarbons and the wear characteristics of the binder and fillers."

Getting the Word Out
Whitford's initial mailing announcing the creation of Xylan explained its attributes this way:

> Our "component formulation" technique permits us to "alloy" a selected fluoropolymer, which provides low friction and release...binders, which impart excellent adhesion and hardness...and a combination of solvents, which permits easy application and quick drying. As application requirements place new emphasis on certain coating qualities, we can modify the formulation to provide qualities you need.

And modify it they did. The first marketable variation on the Xylan theme was soon in the pipeline. Standco Industries, based in Houston, needed a coating for its large nuts and bolts used in the oil and gas industry. Xylan 1010, with its characteristic low friction and excellent release, nonetheless did not provide the needed corrosion resistance. Corrosion inhibitors were added, increasing the coating's resistance fivefold. Xylan 1070 was born.

Thus began a continuous parade of modifications to address specific customer needs:

1410—Low friction, better abrasion, less release
1520—High load, extreme pressure
2440—Best abrasion, slightly lower operating temperature
5000 Series—High performance for small components
8000 Series—High performance for cookware

...and on and on.

One of the most ubiquitous is Xylan 1054, which has been approved for pistons on vehicles worldwide. Among the most noteworthy variations is Xylan 1052, which contains both PTFE and molybdenum disulfide as lubricants, developed in conjunction with Cameron Iron Works and Plastic Applicators in Houston for the Cameron D-body Blowout Preventers. Add specific abrasion reinforcement to 1010, and you have Xylan 1088, which increases abrasion resistance fivefold.

An early mailing listed some of the substrates to which Xylan coatings adhered: four different types of steel; aluminum sheets, bars, rods, and foil; copper, brass, bronze, and other alloys; glass and CorningWare; thermosets like epoxy, polyester, phenolics, and laminates; plastics; wood; and paper.

"These are the ones we know of," the mailing stated. "Because a material is not listed doesn't mean Xylan won't adhere to it, it simply means we don't have any experience with it or don't know about it."

The different applications for the Xylan family of products seem limited only by the creativity of those designing products that require a release coating. They range from the obvious, like consumer cookware and industrial fasteners, to those that are less so: eyeglass frames and dog combs for resistance to the corrosive effects of cleaning chemicals, saw blades for heat resistance, paper guides in printers to channel away static electricity, gynecology instruments to dissipate the cold feeling from the metal.

Xylan coating in fuel cans used in NASCAR racing allows the fuel to flow more freely, thereby reducing a two-can pit stop by 1.5 seconds, an eternity in high-speed auto racing.

The Early Mailings

As the variations on the Xylan theme continued to increase in number, Whitford used its early direct-mail program highlighting these developments to offer clients the specific-requirement/specific-solution approach that became a company hallmark. In a 1977 mailing, Dave Willis wrote:

> We made a public offer in *Housewares* [the predecessor publication to *HomeWorld Business*]. We said that if we don't have the right Xylan coating for your product, we'll create one. We make this offer for two reasons:
>
> - To demonstrate the endless versatility of the many coatings grouped under the Xylan name.
> - To demonstrate our commitment to serve our clients better than anyone else in the market.

Numerous tests bore out the versatility of Xylan's ever-growing family members: 150 million cycles on a rotary seal at temperatures of up to 360 degrees Fahrenheit, a solenoid cycled more than one hundred million times, ninety million better than the nearest competitor. And Whitford could produce Xylan in virtually any color a client wanted.

Long-Term Truck Tests

In early 1973, a Cummins diesel engine, key components of which were sprayed with Xylan, was installed in a tractor operated by a company called Bilkays Express in Farmingdale, New York. Xylan was sprayed on piston skirts, piston rods, wrist pins, and rod bearings. Thus began a three-year test in a vehicle used for delivery service during the day and shuttle operations at night, all of it in a punishing inner-city environment. An identical vehicle, with uncoated components, was also put in service. No single driver was assigned to either truck.

At the close of the three years, with almost two hundred thousand miles on each truck, the one with the coated components had consumed 14.8 percent less fuel. At the time, the National Science Foundation estimated that if all heavy trucks operating in inner-city service could reduce fuel consumption by 15 percent, the country would save 1.5 billion gallons of fuel each year.

Other tests established that Xylan-coated components significantly extended the period between major engine overalls and even reduced diesel engine noise.

Xylan 2525: A Case Study

The auto industry is highly competitive, so companies are always looking for an edge, especially if they can get it by improving production and cutting costs. A revolutionary development at Whitford became front and center in that regard as soon as it hit the marketplace. Designated Xylan 2525, the coating cured via ultraviolet light as opposed to thermal curing in ovens. An immediate market was born: extruded rubber sealing systems used throughout all motor vehicles.

A source emitting UV light at a specified wavelength is directed onto the coated part, which contains a photo-initiator that absorbs the UV light and sets in motion a chemical reaction that converts the liquid formulation into a solid, curing almost instantly. While Xylan 2525 cures in less than one second, thermally cured coatings take five to ten minutes at or above three hundred degrees Fahrenheit.

The benefits are wide ranging: an 80 percent reduction in energy costs, less material waste and the associated disposal costs, adhesion to thermoplastics and other temperature-sensitive substrates. Furthermore, the equipment needed to cure Xylan 2525 is roughly the size of an office desk, as opposed to thermal ovens that averaged ninety feet in length. Slowed by their thermal curing times, the extrusion lines for seals made of ethylene propylene diene monomer (EPDM) that are used throughout motor vehicles, were capable of running five times faster than they had been—that is, Xylan 2525 improved the efficiency of those lines by 500 percent.

Meanwhile, the EU had been adding stricter recycling requirements for the end of a motor vehicle's life. EPDM is not recyclable. As a result, more manufacturers were seeking new ways to produce sealing systems from recyclable thermoplastic materials that degraded in thermal ovens. The UV curing of Xylan 2525 left those beneficial properties intact.

The building industry is another major beneficiary for UV-cured coatings. An article in the April 2004 issue of *European Coatings Journal* put it this way:

> UV-curable coatings are well known within the industry. A significant amount of the coatings used e.g. in the furniture or window industry is cured by UV radiation. One of the most important advantages of UV-curable coatings over conventional air-drying or heat-cured coatings is the speed of cure…Rubber seals play an important role both in the construction of vehicles and buildings. Without them, it is currently impossible to make windows wind and watertight.

The article pointed out that the practice employed at the time for window seals had significant disadvantages:

> On top of acting as a design element, flexible fluoropolymer coatings are used as an assembly aid for window profiles. The rubber seals have to be lubricated before they can be fitted into the window frame. Currently silicone oils are used for this, but this solution suffers from disadvantages. As silicone oils are liquids they tend to contaminate the window glass during the assembly. This leads to extra costs for extensive cleaning. In the case of modern self-cleaning facades, the use of silicone oils is not possible at all as they destroy the self-cleaning property of the glass by attacking the coating on the glass.[10]

The Xylan Soup Stock

Given all its manifestations over time, Xylan even had attributes that were not at first apparent, especially in the early stages of its existence. As it was initially formulated, it was considered unsuitable as a cookware coating and would not stand up to the rigors of stovetop conditions. (See chapter four.) That was later shown to be a rush to judgment.

"At the time, we did not know enough about the cookware business to realize the properties and how they would work," Dave Willis explains. "We missed a huge opportunity out of ignorance. It would not, will not stand up as a topcoat. There are many much better products with much better release. It turns out, however, that with some small modification, it makes a great primer."

---

10 "UV-Cured Coatings," *European Coatings Journal,* April 2004.

What is truly astonishing about the Xylan story is the way it has come to characterize how Whitford operates. Consider that an allegiance to an innovation that sprang to life more than fifty years ago in a tiny lab, before the introduction of so much modern technology that drives innovation today, did not shackle Whitford to the past. It served as the inspiration for an ever more innovative future in which it still plays a central role. And it remains a key player at a worldwide company with all the state-of-the-art technology that is now used to generate new members of Xylan's ever-growing family.

In effect, the development of Xylan created a fluoropolymer soup stock to which combinations of ingredients could be added to achieve a desired recipe. Once this history of successful variations was well established, the possibilities became virtually limitless. New variations for the coating would focus on the needs of customers or prospects. At the same time, however, ever more ingenious variations expanded outward, driven by the resourcefulness of Whitford chemists or the "what if" questions of Whitford management. While "can do" may introduce a single, even revolutionary development at some companies, these words defined the ongoing process of creating products during Whitford's half century. On the other hand, the words "can't be done" were completely foreign to the people at Whitford.

By putting PTFE into a matrix that would form a basis for its usefulness, Xylan was truly transformative. Tests have affirmed that PTFE forms the only known surface to which a gecko cannot stick—a practical test of scientific principle if there ever was one. After decades of adding Xylan atop countless substrates, the only known surface to which *it* will not stick is silicone. It is Xylan's ultimate irony that once it sticks to a surface, nothing else will stick to it. Not even a gecko can manage a foothold.

CHAPTER 18

THAT UNIQUELY WHITFORD WAY

So, if we sell $100 million worth of product, we are on $1 billion worth of the product that's out there."
— JIM GIBIAN, WHITFORD'S WORLDWIDE CONSUMER MARKETING MANAGER

The great irony in what Whitford does is that the company creates surfaces, but its identity is so far below the surface of where its coatings end up that it is almost always invisible to the end user.

"We're responsible for a very small portion of the components in a finished product, a thin layer," explained Jim Gibian, Whitford's worldwide consumer marketing manager. "We're providers of thin film. So the actual amount of our product that ends up on the finished product is a minute amount compared to the overall result. It requires very little material but is responsible for about ten times its contribution to the overall business sale. So, if we sell $100 million worth of product, we are on $1 billion worth of the product that's out there."

While it may be difficult to quantify accurately Whitford's contributions to our lives, it is undeniable that those contributions are real, that they improve our lives. How could you possibly calculate how coatings on cylinders and pistons in millions and millions of vehicles manufactured over many years have reduced the amount of greenhouse gases expelled into the air?

"The automotive and transportation industry is the largest end use application for fluoropolymers," according to a report by MarketsAndMarkets.com, an international research firm. "The growing trend toward lower vehicle weight, lower emissions, and enhanced fuel efficiency is expected to drive the consumption growth of fluoropolymers in the automotive and transportation industry."

In addressing future energy needs, how could you accurately determine the potential for more positive effects of Whitford on the environment, as its coatings become part of the operations of renewable energy wind- and water-powered equipment? Is it a stretch to claim that the efficiency of cookware, bakeware, and other household items on day-to-day living is a stress reducer? How do you judge the impact on your personal well-being of the silence in your car, away from a noisy world, a result of Whitford coatings throughout the vehicle? What about the smoother operation of medical equipment? The strength and efficiency of coated paper? The strength and endurance of textiles?

Creating the improvements in all these areas, however, is the result of a mind-set that celebrates each achievement as just one more step along a never-ending journey, a quest that is endless in itself.

For comedic effect at a company party a number of years ago, Michael Coates, Whitford's worldwide business development manager, wrote an ersatz press release celebrating Whitford's finally creating the ultimate fluoropolymer coating: "Zeroflon, a phenomenal additive, which completely eliminates friction." Unfortunately, the press release went on, the company executive accepting an award for Zeroflon slipped on some, his body bouncing down flights of stairs and coming to rest far down the road.

It can be argued that Whitford's Xylan has gotten as close as could be expected to creating…call it Zeroflon Plus. It's almost impossible to imagine a more slippery coating. Coefficient of friction measurements for Xylan have come in as low as 0.02, the lowest level ever recorded. While CF is a measurement of little accuracy, according to Dave Willis, "we probably are safe with 0.04. Pretty low either way."

Though tongue-in-cheek, Coates's fictional news story about a company finally discovering its Holy Grail nonetheless addresses why a well-run business is never about reaching a destination but about the ongoing journey.

A Business Model?
Is this "Whitford Way" simply uniquely suited to its business, its customers, the skills it requires of its employees? Or is it a business model for other companies as well? The elements of that model, detailed throughout the preceding chapters, would seem transferrable beyond Whitford: continuous personal contact with customers, following those customers wherever they put down roots, creating specific solutions to specific problems, pressing forward even during economic downturns, valuing and empowering employees, rejecting the concept of can't-be-done chemistry, and so on. The elements seem almost intuitively obvious. So

why are some companies "household names but hideous places to work," as one reviewer of a business bestseller wrote? There are many answers to the question, but they require energy better spent on those solutions that are so valued at Whitford.

Many of the best business builders are born to the task. While they have an ever-expanding knowledge base within their chosen fields, an intense drive to overcome challenges and best their competitors, they also possess those indefinable instincts that point them to paths that others do not see. In the process, what they create draws like-minded, can-do people into their fold, people who feel they want to be part of something special, then in turn help create something extraordinary. Any number of people at Whitford, many of them longtime employees, have said, "Once I met Dave Willis, I knew I wanted to work for him." Willis, on the other hand, insists it is those employees who have made Whitford the great success it is today.

Once, in response to an interviewer's question, Willis said, "I guess if enough people keep saying we have done something really special at Whitford, we should start believing it." Time and again, what is most significant about his responses are that they invariably are framed as "Whitford" and "we," as opposed to "I" or "me."

Postscript

Over the years, Dave Willis has demonstrated a particular genius for seeing Whitford products used in some of the most improbable of applications. One of those is paper. (See chapter eleven.) Hence…

"For more years than I care to count, we have been talking about coating paper with PTFE," Willis wrote in an e-mail to staff on October 18, 2016. "Talking, but not doing. We have finally coated and calendared a kraft paper, then put a pressure-sensitive adhesive on the uncoated reverse side. This has provided us with a product aimed (for the moment) at the furniture industry to provide smooth motion on drawer slides. The product looks and feels absolutely appropriate to make wooden drawers slide more easily and uniformly with less or no problems due to changes in humidity."

Willis attached a Whitford bulletin put together for a semiannual trade show in High Point, North Carolina, home base of the furniture industry in the United States, explaining the specific benefits of the product for the wood furniture industry.

The company chose to trademark the product as "GlidePath" solely with the furniture industry in mind but, based on its appearance and feel, it had the potential for many more applications. One major industrial application would be as a separation agent for huge plastic moldings such as fiberglass boats or wind blades with large flat or nearly flat surfaces. The coated fiberglass cloth that is used is expensive. Coated paper could accomplish the same thing at a fraction of the cost.

"My question to you is where else do you see this a useful product?" Willis's e-mail continued. "Touchy feely samples are available for the asking. We can offer samples of nearly any length, but are limited to a width of 10 inches. At the moment we are limiting sales to the United States until we have more experience. What are your ideas? The thoughts so far include uses such as: low- and medium-duty bearings, ready-to-assemble furniture, do-it-yourself rolls to fix the drawers at home, and end-users like Ikea."

As always, ever onward…

Epilogue

Final Thoughts

Over a period of many years, we, at Whitford, have adopted a number of fairly unconventional points of view and "management methods" not endorsed by the managers of more traditional businesses. Here are some final thoughts:

Sales are all important. They drive the company in good times, but even more important in bad times. The competition will cut back making it easier for you to tell your story. Remember, the customer needs new ideas as well.

Profits will follow and increase rapidly after the breakeven point is exceeded so long as the sales are not made at a stupid price just to achieve turnover.

Cutting costs are only marginally useful in gaining profits. More sales are permanent, far outlasting any small reduction in costs. That is not to say one should ignore costs, but they should be given their place, which should not be to replace or especially reduce the cost of sales.

Sales budgets are simply a waste of time, first when they are discussed for hours on end during their preparation by management and sales, then again during the year when reasons (largely excuses) are found as to why the sales are not meeting budget projections. The concept that a budget can be prepared in the fall and go for the ensuing fifteen months is ludicrous. More important are products in the pipeline.

Capital budgets largely imitate the sales budgets. Too much time is taken to get there and the idea of predicting and then limiting the amount to fourteen to fifteen months in the future is absurd. If management agrees that an item is needed, buy it. So what if the decision is made in May?

Research and development should be an ongoing expense in good or lesser times. The time frame involved in most projects exceeds the slow times. New products need to be ready for the next uptick in sales and may help make that happen.

Quality products should be the emphasis of the development efforts. They make it easier for the sales team to tell the story and in time establish "you" as the leader in the category, affording more opportunities to sell and earn the consequent profits.

Fads in business are no more meaningful than they are in clothing. Every few years someone, or some group, comes up with an idea that is decades old, recasts it with a new name, and packages it as new and something that "must" be adopted by all forward-looking companies. *Harvard Business Review* shows this as special skill.

Corporate titles are largely both misleading and limiting. A VP whose job has outgrown him or her as the company has expanded has to be let go. Putting someone over him or her generally causes a morale problem among all close associates. A senior manager can be "assisted" by someone who may be senior, but not obnoxiously so.

Communications. Bear in mind in an international company English is not the first language of many of the recipients of correspondence. Brief messages will be read. Long messages will not. Being concise is a virtue and having to reduce the volume may give you a clearer insight into the entire subject. Much over a single page is seldom read in its entirety.

Final, final thought. There is nothing more foolish than cutting travel to save money. In good times or poor, the customer may need help. If you intend to be in business for the years to come, spend money now. We have a competitor that banned its tech service people from flying. In the couple of years until the policy was changed, our people did the tech service for the competitor's customer. It is now our multi-million dollar account.

David P. Willis, February 2017

Endpaper

In Defiance of Convention

Endpaper: a sheet of paper, often distinctively colored or ornamented, folded vertically once to form two leaves, one of which is pasted flat to the inside of the front or back cover of a book, with the other pasted to the inside edge of the first or last page to form a flyleaf.
— DICTIONARY.COM

No vertical fold here. Not pasted to either the back cover or the inside edge of the last page. Not distinctly colored or ornamented. Instead, a photograph and some text. Defiance of convention.

The photograph was taken on March 7, 2015, at a celebration of Whitford's fiftieth anniversary, in the ballroom of the Hyatt Regency in downtown Chicago, the first night of the annual International Home + Housewares Show at McCormick Place. It depicts a gathering of Whitford personnel from its departments in the US and locations throughout the world, all representative of essential elements in the Whitford business formula. That the collection of individuals in the photo follows no preconceived lineup of the corporate hierarchy is itself representative of Whitford's long-established flaunting of convention.

The food and drink, the music, the performance by Whitford staff members, while perhaps not unusual at a golden anniversary celebration, playing hard is a long established tradition at Whitford. "They are the only people I know who have negotiated a flat rate at the hotel bar," said one of the company's many customers in attendance that evening.

Next day it was back to work at the booth, in the meeting rooms, in hospitality suites, at impromptu gatherings on the floor of the convention center; addressing customer needs, challenges, problems with those uniquely Whitfordesque solutions. The transition into the next half-century.

Index

A

Abrasion, 115-121, 160, 167, 262-263
Acid Test, 54
Advanced Flexible Composites (AFC), 233
Advertising, 51, 79, 192-209
　In-House Agency, 52, 197-199, 205
Akzo Nobel, 231-232
All-Clad, 251, 258
Alchemy, 91, 106-107
Allergan, 240
Alpha Coatings, 111-117
Ambiente housewares show, 142-143, 221
Annas, Christopher, 64, 69-74, 235, 243
Automotive Metal, 109

B

BP, 126, 129
Badner, John, 77-79, 149-152
Bakeware, numerous references throughout the text
Bearings, 20, 36, 121, 164-165, 264, 273
Becherplast, 153-154, 231
Berry, Gareth, 132-137
Bilkays Express, 264-265
BlisterGuard, 166-167
Bock, Laszlo, 11
Boerner, Miriam, 223, 226
Brazil, 60, 62, 117, 119, 144, 228, 230, 232, 240
Brescia, Italy, 154, 239
British Nuclear Fuels (BNF), 92
Bruker testing machine, 122
Bundt Pan, 148-149
Bureau of Labor Statistics (US), 20
Burger Maker, 64
Burns, Darlee, 169
Butler, Stephen, 117

281

C

Cameron Iron Works, 126, 263
Canada, 56, 62, 234, 240, 252
Chan, Jackie, 86
Cheng, Stanley, 146
Chevron, 126
Chicago, Illinois, 60, 77, 143, 247, 280
China, 61-62, 84, 144-145, 158-160, 186, 232, 236, 240, 242
    Jiangmen, 61, 158
    Ningbo, 158
    Pearl River Delta, 61
    Shanghai, 158
Clairol, 72, 80-82, 87, 199
Coates, Michael, 114, 228, 237, 270-271
Colombia, 62, 144, 239-240
Cookware, numerous references throughout the text
Cooper Standard Automotive, 115
Cookware Manufacturers Association (CMA), 105, 161
Corrosion, numerous references throughout the text
Crest Coatings, 245-246, 259
Cummins Diesel, 264
Curtain Coating, 176-178, 184-185
Customer Lifetime Value (CLV), 244-245

D

Daigle, Sandra, 251-252
Daily Telegraph, 32
Dalquist, Henry and Dotty, 148
Darner, Leif, 232
DiMaggio, Joe, 64
Direct Mail, 24, 52, 59, 192, 195, 203, 209
DiSalvo, Mario, 250-251, 258
Disney, Walt, 16
Dollar General, 65
Dow Jones, 73
Doyle, Arthur Conan, 108
Drucker, Peter, 192
DuPont, numerous references throughout the text

E

Eberhardt, Joan, 150, 152, 199, 206, 217, 221
Eberhardt, Suzie, 245
Eclipse, 201
Edge, Dr. Gordon, 133
Elverson, Pennsylvania, 16, 19, 102, 110, 168, 186, 228
Engineering Design Guide, 206-208
Entrepreneur, 1, 23, 111
Epoxy, 171-173, 263
Erickson, Mike, 246, 259
Eterna, 106
EterniTex, 167
Ethylene propylene diene monomer (EPDM), 266
European Coatings Journal, 266
European Marine Energy Centre (EMEC), 134-137
European Marketing Program, 156

European Union (EU), 132, 134, 156-157, 236-237, 266
Excalibur Coating System, 78, 98-99, 197, 199
ExxonMobil, 126, 140

F
Fabrics, 4, 166-167, 233
Family Dollar, 65
Farberware, 79
Fastener Technology magazine, 203
Federal Corporate Average Fuel Economy (CAFE) standards, 118
Ferguson, Herb, 254-255
Ferro Corporation, 82
Fields, Charlie, 118-119, 169, 211, 226
Fields, Paul, 12, 25, 36-44, 47, 72, 90, 107, 226
Financial Times, 32
Flexible Finishes, 109, 114, 117
Flint, Ted, 172-173
Fluoropolymer, numerous references throughout the text
Fluorinated ethylene propylene (FEP), 33-34, 40, 169
Fombio, Italy, 232
Ford, 4, 89, 113, 116, 118
Fostoria, Ohio, 111
France, 62, 132, 156, 240
Freon, 39-40
Friction, numerous references throughout the text

Coefficient of, 118, 133, 160, 271
Fry Pans, 64-65, 106, 158, 193, 199
Furniture, 4, 165, 234, 273

G
Galafassi, Antonio, 189-190
Garnett, Martin, 121
Gates, Bill, 255
GE Oil and Gas, 126
General Electric, 230
General Motors, 4, 113, 115
George Foreman Grill, 82-87
Germany, 13, 60, 62, 112, 142, 156, 220, 222-223, 240-241
Gibian, Jim, 144-145, 183-184, 269
Giannetti, Peter, 200
GlidePath, 273
Global Management Team, 213
Goldman Sachs, 125
Google, 11
Gretzky, Wayne, 75
Groesbeck, Fran (Attilio), 77-79, 149-153, 156, 200-201
Guelph, Ontario, 234
Guide to Corporate Communications, 208

H
Halliburton, 126
Harms, Ken, 249-250
Harvard Business Review, 8, 9, 180, 191, 276

283

Harvey, Dr. Leonard, 91-94, 239
Hayward, Barbara (Ficca), 67-68, 217
Hell's Kitchens, 197-199
Henniges Automotive, 115
HomeWorld Business, 157-158, 199, 200, 264
Honda, 115
Hong Kong, 60-62, 66, 73, 83, 146, 158, 216, 228, 240
Hoover, 32
Houston, Texas, 50, 59, 69, 87, 126, 128, 188-189, 262-263
HP Polymers, 234
HP Zenker, 156
Hutchinson, 115
Hwaseung R&A Automotive Parts Co, 115
Hyundai, 4, 115

I
India, 11, 62, 144-145, 158, 212-213, 232, 240
International Home + Housewares Show (Chicago), 77, 143, 280
International Organization for Standardization (ISO), 169-170
Industrial Valley Bank (IVB), 69-71
Italy, 62, 153-156, 178, 231-232, 239-240

J
Japan, 62
Jones, Tracy, 100-101
James, Geoffrey, 8
James Neil, 32
Jarrett, Delores "Dee", 219-220, 224-225
Jung-Deisel, Stephanie, 222

K
Kassulke, Sandra (Quinn), 215-218, 226
Keystone College, 43
Kia, 4
Kinugawa Rubber Industrial, 115
Kissling, Tim, 249-250, 258
Klutke, Marcel, 253, 258
Kneadatite, 173-174
Kodak, 166
Krauss, Clifford, 125

L
Lee, Richard, 83-84, 86
Leech, Larry, 47-48, 66, 72, 230
Lifetime Brands, 183
Liquid Nitrogen Processing (LNP), 2, 20, 22-24, 26, 35, 45, 48, 50, 57, 182
Linde India, 213
Los Angeles, California, 60

M
Machine Design, 202

Macy's, 77-79, 86, 149, 151
Magna International, 115
Manchester, United Kingdom, 31
Manhattan Project, 37
March, Susan, 219
MarketsAndMarkets.com, 270
Marshall, Colin, 254
Mather Fluorotech, 37
McCulloch-Williams, Martha, 142, 161
McDonald's, 204
Mecray, Kurt, 91, 95-96, 111, 147-148, 151-152, 186
Medical Coatings, 89, 168-171, 179, 211, 226, 270
Melt Flow, 66, 71-72, 88, 147
Melville, Andrew, 117, 119
Mercedes-Benz, 4, 115
Meridian Bank, 65, 74, 235
Meyer (Mai-Yah) Manufacturing, 66-67, 74, 79, 88, 146-147, 256
Miller, Mike, 93, 101-105, 152, 187-188, 253
Mirro Cookware, 189-190
Mr. Coffee, 64-65
Multitop, 83

N
NASCAR, 263
National Science Foundation, 265
Neely, Peter, 211-212, 216
Nesbitt, Bruce, 247-248, 258
Netherlands, 60
New York Times, 125
Nissan, 4, 115
National Presto, 64-65
Nordic Ware, 147-148
North Sea, 132
Northland Aluminum Products, 148-149
Norway, 131-132

O
Occam's Razor, 33, 37-38, 44
Ogilvy & Mather, 51, 193
Oil Patch, 59, 86-88, 126, 140, 188
Opening Price Point products (OPP), 65
Orion Industries, 247, 258
Orkney Islands, Scotland, 134, 137
Owens Corning Fiberglas, 19-20

P
Paper coating, 163-166, 179, 207, 234, 263, 270, 272-273
Paris Climate Agreement, 124-125, 129, 140
Parkes, Debbie, 174-175
Pathak, Sanjoy, 212-213, 226
Pearl River Delta, China, 61
Pehoviak, Chris, 221-222, 226
Penn State University, 96
Pennwalt Corporation, 25-27, 45, 220
Peppers, Don, 244

Peters, Thomas J., 76
Pfund, Nancy, 125
Pfizer, 240
Phi Gamma Delta fraternity, 20, 29
Phillips Petroleum, 65-67, 69, 71-72, 74, 88, 147, 256
Pinter, Michael, 115-116
Polyamideimide (PAI), 33-34
Polymer, 66, 91, 164, 175, 207, 233-234, 260-261
Polymeric Systems, Inc. (PSI), 171
Polytetrafluoroethylene (PTFE), numerous references throughout the text
Powell, John, 29-32, 39, 60, 68, 80, 230
Precision Coating Technology and Manufacturing (PCTM), 249-250
Product Finishing magazine, 203

Q
Quality Control (QC), 14, 79, 89, 100-101, 172, 185, 255
QuanTanium, 201
Quantum2, 77, 149

R
Recession, 10, 20, 73
Rehmeyer, Ted, numerous references throughout the text
Reilly, Amy, 256
Reinhold Industries Ltd, 253, 258
Renault

Research and Development (R&D), numerous references throughout the text
Resilon, 111-113, 123
Restriction of Hazardous Substances (RoHS) standards, 122
Retail Marketing Program, 152-153, 156
Reynolds, Andy, 156-157
Rice Cookers, 5, 157-159
Rochester, New York, 60
Rogers, Martha, 244
Roller Coatings, 176
Rubber Coatings, 26, 35, 56, 109, 111, 114-115, 117, 265-267
Runcorn, Cheshire, United Kingdom, 30, 121, 212, 230, 233
Russo, John, 97-100, 109, 122, 176-179
Ryals, Lynette, 8-9

S
SaarGummi Group, 115
Sales, numerous references throughout the text
    Inside, 8-10, 86, 128, 188-189, 254, 260
    Outside, 8-10, 182, 188-189
Salton Corporation, 84
Schuette, Tim, 111-114
Schultz, Jill, 214-215, 226
Scotland, 29, 134

Scrabble, 53
Sealynx, 115
Seitzinger, Ron, 49, 249-250
Shell Oil Company, 126
Siegel, Spencer, 165-167
Silo Mentality, 237
Singapore, 62, 151, 158, 215-217, 230-231, 240-241
Smith, Craig, 127
Society of the Plastics Industry (SPI), 24, 27, 46
Spain, 60, 62, 156, 240
Sprayed Coatings, 98, 176, 197, 255, 264
Standco Industries, 262
Standard Profil, 115
Sun Belt Coatings, 251
Sun Plastics, 49
Suzuki, 4, 115
Svanberg, Carl-Henric, 129
Switzerland, 60, 169, 241

T
Taiwan, 26, 83-84
Taxes, 31, 240, 242
Tetran, 159
Tidal Energy, 133-139
TK China, 84
Toastmaster, 84
Toyoda Gosei, 115
Toyota, 4, 115
Tramontina USA, 189-190
Turkey, 62, 240

U
Ultraviolet light (Cured Coatings), 160, 265
Union Carbide, 50
United Kingdom (UK), numerous references throughout the text
United States Travel Association (USTA), 9-10
University of Delaware, 42
University of Liverpool, 92
University of Pennsylvania, 19-20, 180, 230, 244
Wharton School, 19, 29, 180-181, 244
Urban Dictionary, 238

V
Vallaperta, 154-155
 Attilio, 154
 Francesco, 154
 Giuseppe (Chicco), 155, 232
Venturi Effect, 92
Vietnam, 62, 144, 158-159, 240
Volatile Organic Compounds (VOC), 175, 257
Volkswagen, 4, 115

W
Wall Street Journal, 32, 159
Walton, Sam, 244
Waterman, Robert H., 76
Wave Power, 133-139

Weir, Tony, 51-52, 54-55, 68, 150, 152, 192-194, 197-199, 202-204, 208-210
West Chester, Pennsylvania, 19, 23, 69, 235
Wies, Simone, 222
Whitcon, 39
White, Terry, 111
Whitford Chemical, 2, 23-25, 33, 35, 45, 172, 219, 220
Whitford Country Club, 22
Whitford Flexible Composites (WFC), 233-234
Whitford GmbH, Germany, 60, 222
Whitford Plastics Ltd (WPL), United Kingdom, 30, 60, 121, 211, 230
Whitford University, 185-186, 251, 253
Whitford Worldwide Company, 60-62, 75, 91, 181, 228, 242, 260
Wikipedia, 163

Willis, Anne, 213, 217-223, 235-237, 239
Willis, Brian, 7, 9-10, 87-88, 128, 139-140, 188, 261
Willis, David P. (Dave), numerous references throughout the text
Final Thoughts, 275
Wind Power, 5, 88, 124-125, 129-130, 132-136, 138-139, 234, 270, 273
Wilson, Harold, 30
Wong, Philip, 158, 160
Work Hard/Play Hard, 13-14, 23, 93, 238,
Wu, T.K., 84

X

Xomox Corporation, 27-28, 56, 182
Xylan, numerous references throughout the text

Z

Zeroflon, 271